DRUGS AND THE OTHER SELF

DRUGS | An
AND THE | Anthology
OTHER | of Spiritual
SELF | Transformations

edited with an introduction
by
CHAMAN NAHAL

PERENNIAL LIBRARY
Harper & Row, Publishers, Inc.,
New York

To
MY AMERICAN STUDENTS
who are an excellent lot
and a challenge all the time

DRUGS AND THE OTHER SELF

Introduction, editorial notes, and compilation copyright
© 1971 by Chaman Nahal.

First PERENNIAL LIBRARY edition published 1971.

Library of Congress Catalog Card Number: 79-146802

CONTENTS

Passages in the book are taken from the following sources:

1. *The Hasheesh Eater,* by Fitz Hugh Ludlow (New York: Harper & Brothers, 1857).

2. *Annual Report of the Smithsonian Institution, 1897* (Washington: Government Printing Press, 1898).

3. *The Doors of Perception,* by Aldous Huxley (New York: Harper & Row, 1954).

4. *Mysticism: Sacred and Profane,* by R. C. Zaehner (Oxford: Clarendon Press, 1957).

5. *Exhumations,* by Christopher Isherwood (London: Methuen & Co., 1966).

6. *Studies in Personality* by McNemar and Merrill (New York: McGraw-Hill, 1962).

7. *Les Paradis Artificiels,* by Charles Baudelaire, translated by Arthur Symons (London: The Casanova Press, 1925).

8. *The Knickerbocker,* July 1842.

9. *A Conversation With J. Krishnamurti,* by C. L. Nahal (New Delhi: Arya Book Depot, 1965).

10. *Essays,* First Series, by Ralph Waldo Emerson (Cambridge: Riverside Press, 1883).

ACKNOWLEDGMENTS

Grateful acknowledgment is made by the author to all the following for permission to use copyright material.

Arya Book Depot, New Delhi, for reprinting a chapter from my book *A Conversation With J. Krishnamurti*.

Casanova Press, London, for reprinting a section from *Les Paradis Artificiels* by Charles Baudelaire.

Clarendon Press, Oxford, for reprinting a section from *Mysticism: Sacred and Profane* by R. C. Zaehner.

Francoise Delisle, for reprinting *Mescal: A New Artificial Paradise* by Havelock Ellis.

Harper & Row, Publishers, Inc., New York, and Chatto and Windus Ltd., London, for reprinting passages from *The Doors of Perception* by Aldous Huxley.

McGraw-Hill Book Company, New York, for reprinting "Mechanisms of Hallucinations" from *Studies in Personality* by McNemar & Merrill. Copyright 1962.

Simon & Schuster, Inc., New York, and Curtis Brown Ltd., London, for reprinting a section from *Exhumations* by Christopher Isherwood.

PREFACE

The enigma of human personality is ever intriguing. If our physical existence and our moods can be oriented by what we eat and drink, why not by drugs? And what of the use of drugs to achieve salvation or nirvana? How far is it possible or justifiable to extend human consciousness through external stimuli? The material offered here attempts to provide a line of thought to these queries.

In my generalizations, I have drawn exclusively on the experiences of people with a mature sensibility. Here it is hoped that the book differs from other presentations, which tend to be based on the accounts of juvenile drug users.

Princeton, N.J.   Chaman Nahal
1970

Section I ‖ INTRODUCTION

The Drug Phenomenon

Narcotics cannot still the Tooth
That nibbles at the soul—
—*Emily Dickinson*

The most remarkable phenomenon of the sixties was the widespread employment of drugs for mind expansion, or what Dr. Timothy Leary has called "biochemical mysticism." This demonstrates how acutely most people felt the need for something beyond them, a power, a force maybe—a unit of energy at one time designated by that outmoded word "God." In an age where the theorists tell us "God is dead," delivering neat little lectures to that effect in undergraduate seminars, this manifestation is in some respects a heartening development.

For the last fifty years, until these indigenous or synthetic chemical substances came on the scene, the prevailing cry of the century was one of despair. The first World War shattered the illusion of progress under which modern Europe had lived since the Renaissance. It seemed that civilizations did not continue on an endless path of success; rather, they moved in cycles. Historians like Spengler and Toynbee were on hand to substantiate this and offer proof. Spengler in *The Decline of the West* even said that so far as the present European civilization was concerned, it had exhausted itself and was in a state of rapid disintegration. And Toynbee came up with very nearly same conclusion in *A Study of History*. The two wars, in which millions perished and in which so many "civilized" nations were involved, were living proof of that decline.

From the twenties onward, the literature of most European countries has repeatedly reflected this spirit of despair. *The Waste Land,* symbolic poem of the century, is a poem without hope. Kafka's *The Trial* and *The Castle,* Aldous Huxley's *Ape and Essence,* Orwell's *1984,* while at one level representing localized situations, are essentially products of fear, a joylessness of the spirit. When Gertrude Stein said of her contemporaries, "You are all a lost generation," she had quite a point.

Add to this the extreme materialism of communism, the extreme negation of Freudian psychology, and the extreme objectivity of the physical sciences, and our picture of the dethronement of God is complete. It had been coming ever since Hobbes and Locke, but no one expected quite such an absolute finish. Under communism, the poor chap couldn't have survived a day; they were too busy redistributing land and property to bother about him. Freud systematically reduced him to a bogeyman, the product of early fears and inhibitions, mostly sexual, who like the ghost of Julius Caesar before Brutus vanished the moment one put libido in order and looked him in the face ("Now I have taken heart thou vanishest"). As for the sciences, they had long since dispensed with him. They demanded proof— verifiable proof—the kind of mathematical proof that landed Neil Armstrong and Edwin Aldrin on the moon on July 20, 1969.

One might have imagined that after all this, man would be happy on earth. Religions had been the opium of people and now these religions were exposed. A good time was coming, was even now at hand—so the glad tidings again seemed to run. For some years people were so carried away by the new philosophy that they shook hands with each other saying, "God is dead," as once they used to say, "Good morning." If one's religious affiliation was mentioned at all, it was done apologetically.

But one thing the current drug phenomenon has effected is to re-establish the validity of God. While it does not seem proper for God to, as it were, sneak in again through the back door, after what He suffered at our hands perhaps He had no other choice. Drugs have, if nothing else, shown man up: the myth of man as master of the world, his pitiable claims to knowing the answers to everything, his boastful dependence on technology, the haughty arrogance with which he dismissed the supernatural— none of these has brought him peace and contentment or a sense of completion. Man is, as he has always been, an incomplete being, and his greatest search is still for something beyond the phenomenal world, without which that world remains an imperfect abstraction. To say this is to praise not drugs but the fact that in their own ironic fashion drugs have once again brought to light man's basic spiritual needs.

It is customary to speak of drug use as "addiction." The term in its Latin form *addicere* meant the excessive involvement of a person or thing with another. Only in recent times have we commonly used it to refer to a person in thrall to drugs. Addiction thus has become the scarlet letter of the age, and is being used to beat the innocent, the guilty, and the unwary.

But what is the man (or woman) who turns to drugs so frequently trying to do or say? Very briefly, he is unhappy; very briefly, he is doing something he thinks will bring him happiness.

In his search for happiness, the user of drugs is no different from the countless others who in their own way have attempted the same thing. This is a world full of misery. Children are born with defects. Healthy bodies are suddenly stricken and perish. As loved ones grow old, they become hateful. Our ambitions are only partially realized, and success may come but seldom satisfaction. Millions live without sufficient food; thousands are killed each year in wars. Famines, earthquakes, hurricanes strike without warning and take their toll. The list of moral evils, of corruption, lechery, the exploitation of man by man, is endless. What is all this for?

It was this question that Prince Siddhartha pondered before he left his father's kingdom to take up the life of a monk. Christ and Muhammad, and other prophets in many lands, were beset by similar doubts before the dawn of their own faiths. The ultimate aim of the teachings of all religious thinkers was to help man achieve a sense of perfection. The visible world was a vale of sorrow; but with something added, it *could* take on the look of beauty.

Where religions and "biochemical mysticism" part company is that the happiness or extension of mind conceived by formal religions rests on the principle of self-denial, as opposed to the self-indulgence that the use of drugs (or other stimuli) involves.

It is quite a moral dilemma, this debate between self-indulgence and self-denial. No one today would approve the excessive mortification of the flesh practiced by the early Christians. The Buddha affirmed centuries ago that excessive self-denial becomes a form of self-indulgence itself, and he vigorously opposed such behavior. In his search for truth he had tried everything: fasting, overeating, living like a recluse, socializing, endless meditation, yoga exercises. Finally he concluded that excess in any one direction was an indulgence. A kick might be there, some kind of satisfaction, but one never broke through the prison wall to reach the sky; there was no real illumination for the self in this sort of process. (Hence his famous doctrine of the middle path.)

The true self-denial posed by religions is a very subtle concept, involving a limited amount of suffering by choice. Loving your neighbor. Chastity. Turning the other cheek. No covetousness. Purity of speech. Humility. Charity. Compassion. Forgiveness rather than sitting in judgment. Occasional silence, occasional abstinence from other wants. These are virtues developed and promoted by man by preference; he knows they do not exist in the rest of the world. The biological life around us seizes what it wants (biological life at least maintains a balance in its wants; man in his indulgences can stoop lower). But for man to be a man, he has to be aware that he can rise above the biological world, and this spiritual realization lies first in the progression from his animal state to that of man, proper man. All religions have seen this clearly, and, making the maximum de-

mands on the priest since he was a servant of the
church, they have laid varying degrees of restraints
upon all other individuals.

The second very important point which all developed religions stress is that the awareness of the self,
a spiritual awakening or any genuine mystic experience, is of a nature that is totally *new;* it is a vision
we cannot compare to anything known by us. In the
life story of each religious teacher, we hear of the
definitive moment when illumination came: to the
Buddha, to Christ, to Muhammad, to Ramakrishna.
We use terms like enlightenment, or the coming of
the light, since human vocabulary cannot adequately
describe such visions. But it is taken for granted that
this illumination is the arrival of a comprehension
absolutely unique and outside natural or general
human experience.

This is probably why no religious teacher has ever
been able to describe his visions coherently. They involve a personal, highly exclusive state of consciousness, which the experiencer alone can understand.
When these masters later described their visions to
their disciples they did so in parables or anecdotes;
and, though they alluded to their experience, never
once did they describe what that experience was. No
one to this day knows precisely what happened to
the Buddha under the bo tree in Gaya or to Christ
when he went up the mountain or into the wilder-
ness.

The third and final difference between genuine
and spurious extensions of the mind is that in genuine mysticism, once the extension does take place,
once the supreme awakening does come about, it

transforms not only the individual but the entire physical universe surrounding him. In a highly metaphorical sense, we have the miracles of conventional religions. If Christ could walk on water, it was only because water too had changed with the enlightenment of Christ and was now acting according to a different set of physical laws. When Ramakrishna could hold his breath for hours in smadhi, with no heartbeat, no movement of the lungs, the whole cosmos was functioning differently and the heart and lungs had to obey. While all this sounds highly improbable, by making such claims these religions at least establish a standard by which true mysticism should be measured. There is a sequence behind these declarations which has a logic of its own. If you do claim to have reached a paradise through your experience, then that paradise must act up to your presence in the same heightened manner that you claim for it. If on the other hand in your heightened state of awareness you step out of the window and the air refuses to hold you up so that you fall seven floors below to your death, there is not much substance to your paradise.

To sum up, the three aspects of a genuine mystical experience, to my mind, are: (1) that it is achieved by the participant through self-denial; (2) that it transforms not only the individual but the entire physical world in relation to that individual; and (3) that it unfolds before the individual a vision so new that it cannot be compared to anything already known by him. In the extension of mind brought about by drugs, in "biochemical mysticism" that is, *all these three aspects are missing*. Taking drugs is a process involving self-indulgence; instead of being master of the desire, one becomes a slave to it. In the experiences produced by these drugs, while the individual consciousness can conceivably be altered for short periods, the rest of the universe takes not the slightest note of that alteration and continues on its course in its normal manner. And finally, the experiences engendered by drugs are never a manifestation of the totally new—even within the limited confines of the individual.

As it happens, the first two of these features are socially restrictive, too. Any self-indulgence can be permitted only to the extent that it does not interfere with the rights of others. Thus, in a heightened state of awareness one is not in command of one's body and may become a hazard to other members of the community.

In this case, however, to a large extent the society itself is to be blamed for what is happening. For the last ten years, Western society in general, and American society in particular, has become more and more permissive. "Wait for the lotus to stir," says D. H. Lawrence in his masterpiece *The Man Who Died,* suggesting that there is a rhythm in the heavens which in due course will take care of our physical needs and we had better not hurry to upset that rhythm. But today sixth graders are given illustrated lectures on orgasm in the name of progress, and modern mothers often put their fifteen-year-old daughters on the pill. The son of the proprietor of a gas station near my home is unable to pass his high school exams; yet the boy drives a new Camaro, and his father boasts that he has four guns and eight pairs of shoes. The life of a student was always considered one of asceticism. He had to prove his mettle before he could reap the pleasures of life. But university students in America today enjoy all types of physical luxury. While they are second to none as scholars, in such an indulgent society what is left ethically or morally for them to aspire to or work for?

The five extracts of drug experiences included in this book bear witness to the fact that the individual loses considerable control of his reflexes after the drug has been assimilated. Aldous Huxley is the most optimistic and lucid of the five in recalling what happened to him. Not only does he note that "the ability to remember and to 'think straight' is little if at all reduced," but he says that the mind's control over the body and the relationship of the body to other material objects is not significantly altered. But the experiences of the others do not corroborate that. Whenever there was mobility, it was far more cumbersome in terms of distance and maneuverability. Havelock Ellis dealt with this by remaining stationary; on the two occasions when he took mescalin, we find him lying down on a couch, for, he says, the slightest movement on his part "had the effect of dispelling the colors," as though mobility were an unwanted factor in such a state. Ludlow found a "merciless stretch of space before him" when moving: the nearest lamppost on the road "seemed separated from me by leagues." Christopher Isherwood's namesake also found movement and coordination difficult; and Zaehner found it hard to control his laughter, even though he knew he was making a spectacle of himself.

One question often posed is whether taking drugs can promote creativity. Heightened feelings, perhaps. Heightened awareness of color and sound, perhaps. But could one sit down and transmute such experiences into literature, painting or composing music while under the influence of drugs? There is the unsubstantiated report that Coleridge wrote both *The Rime of the Ancient Mariner* and *Kubla Khan* under the sway of laudanum (an opium tincture made with alcohol). Coleridge himself never said anything about the former; of the composition of *Kubla Khan* he has left two contradictory versions. In the one where he does refer to opium, I think he is emphasizing the "reverie" or drowsy state it induced; he does not attribute his images to opium. And even if he was inspired by those laudanum dreams, it is difficult to imagine that he actually composed or wrote the poem while on an opium "trip." The same applies to other writers in situations where their creativity has been attributed to drugs. At least half the process of composition consists of physical labor, and any coordinated labor, whether holding a pen or typing while under the influence of a drug, seems well nigh impossible judging by the accounts contained in this book.

Perhaps the greatest damage in this respect has been done by De Quincey's *The Confessions of An English Opium-Eater*. De Quincey wrote his book in 1821 to preach the evils of opium. But most of the time he is unwittingly praising the drug—and praising it in superlatives. Many educated people must have been attracted to drugs because of the enticing tone of this book, in which De Quincey shows how, starting in 1804, for the first eight years off and on, and then for the next ten years every single day, he continued to take opium and come to no harm. The last phase of his life, when he was obliged to quit the habit because his hallucinations were becoming increasingly unbearable, he slurs over. "At length I grew afraid to sleep, and I shrank from it as from the most savage torture." There is a clear sigh of relief when at last he informs us of how he managed his "escape" from the drug. But the revulsion and his rejection are recorded all too briefly, and the reader is more likely to be influenced by the earlier pages about the "pleasures" of opium. It is obviously a case of an artist's rhetoric running away with his reason.

Of course, there are records from earliest times of various races possessing the knowledge of hallucinogenic drugs, and particularly of opium and hashish. As early as 1500 B.C. the Egyptians knew how to collect poppy juice by scraping off the poppy capsule, and by the seventh century B.C. full knowledge of the production and use of opium existed in many lands, including Greece. Theophrastus, a disciple of Aristotle, mentions the method in the fourth century B.C. Dioscorides in the first century A.D. goes on to distinguish the different varieties of poppies that had come to flourish by then. Pliny and Celsus, around the same time, repeat that information.

As far as the literati are concerned, apparently many of them seem to have known of opium. Homer refers to it as the Cup of Helen, which induces forgetfulness and freedom from pain. Virgil mentions it in the *Aeneid*. Chaucer, Shakespeare and Milton all refer to it in their works, and Bacon makes a veiled allusion to it in his *Essays* while dismissing the Turks for their lax morals.

In Eastern texts not only the stimulant but the stimulant giver too is praised. Omar Khayyám in his Rubáiyát was only speaking of wine; but his *saki*, the female cup-filler, gains as much attention from him as the wine ("Ah, Beloved, fill the cup that clears/ Today of past regrets and future fears"). In the Vedas, the scriptural book of the Hindus, many hymns are addressed to an elixir called soma— "Soma, our Friend, heaven's prop and stay"—which was taken in the form of a juice, but which from another phrase ("the sacred grass") in all probability was hashish; in addition to soma, the soma pressers, those who pressed the juice out of the grass, are also venerated.

This familiarity with drugs, however, in no way betokens their widespread use as narcotics. The most extensive praise of a drug in classical times exists in the Vedas, since there are many references to soma by name, and Book IX of the *Rig Veda* is almost exclusively devoted to it. The drink must have been of a very mild variety to win sacramental approval (like the liqueur brewed by Benedictine monks with official approval) and, further, it was conceived of more as a food for the gods, for Indra and others, than for the common people. But it was a drug nonetheless and must have been consumed by human beings. The essential point, however, is that even in the Vedas, it is the inferior hymns that are addressed to soma; the finer hymns, like "The Song of Creation," not only make no mention of it but also implicitly dismiss it by emphasizing inner awarenesses.

By the beginning of the nineteenth century, nevertheless, the use of drugs as stimuli had become quite widespread—"immense," as De Quincey puts it. He tells how in the city of Manchester, when he was young, "on a Saturday afternoon the counters of the druggists were strewed with pills of one, two, or three grains, in preparation for the known demand of the evening." De Quincey saw this as purely an economic issue. The factory workers of Manchester opted for opium because it was cheaper than "ale or spirits." Things have changed much since then. While comparative figures in Manchester are not available, a glassine bag of heroin, a derivative of opium, today sells for $5 (the "nickel bag") in Times Square, whereas draft beer in the same area is only 15¢ a glass. Furthermore, boys and girls of twelve and thirteen have come to act as pushers, even taking the drug themselves and becoming addicted to it. The story of drugs has indeed led us to the very heart of Dante's inferno!

But what of the unknown, the release of the body into the spirit of the universe, the freedom from time and space, the great liberation? It is here that the drugs seem to betray us. High school or college students are attracted to drugs in a spirit of bravado, as they might be attracted to tobacco or their first drink. Broken homes and unhappy family backgrounds also drive many of these youngsters to drugs. But control at this level looks to me to be relatively easy. We should liberalize the laws concerning possession of drugs, as Margaret Mead has so convincingly argued; PTA's and guidance counselors could help paint an effective picture of human potential and the purpose of education; and parents, for a change, could try to bring about the happiness of the entire family, rather than concentrating on their own separate (and selfish) wants.

The warning to youngsters against taking drugs invariably comes from people older than themselves; what they hear from youngsters of their own age is usually an invitation to license. It is essential therefore that the argument against drugs be also advanced by their own peers. To wean the drug addict, the schools will need the services of former drug users; they alone can get through to the others. But more pressing is the need to keep any more children from falling victim to the habit. Most drug pushers tend to be reckless of their personal safety, and since other children want to avoid a fight or public embarrassment, they give in to them. It should not be difficult for any school organization to find children opposed to drugs by conviction. These youngsters should be further instructed about drugs, so that they can win the uninitiated to their position.

But what of the adults, who turn to drugs to escape from emotional privation, or in search of "paradise"? Life is perfect for none of us, and even the most successful have sorrows which at times are too heavy to bear. Sometimes there are physical reasons for this sense of imprisonment: a disease, a deformity; but often the cause is psychological. A feeling of incompleteness breeds an inner ache for which there may be no remedy, unless somehow a way can be found to release the spirit from this physical bondage.

And what kind of release do drugs offer a person who seeks their embrace? Of the people represented here, the only one who addresses himself philosophically to this subject is Aldous Huxley. In *Mysticism: Sacred and Profane,* R. C. Zaehner was extremely unfair to Huxley when he tried to classify him along with "profane" mystics. I entirely agree with Zaehner that drugs cannot take one into a true mystic experience. His own experiment with mescalin, during which nothing of any significance happened to him, is included here. But when he challenges the premise of Huxley's experience and tries to debunk his phraseology, he is on dangerous ground.

First, Huxley nowhere in *The Doors of Perception* states that what he experienced when he took fourtenths of a gram of mescalin in 1953 was a "mystic" experience. Rather he declares very clearly, "I am not so foolish as to equate what happens under the influence of mescalin or of any other drug, prepared or in the future preparable, with the realization of the end and ultimate purpose of human life: Enlightenment, the Beatific Vision." What mescalin does, according to Huxley, is to make you aware of the metaphysical problem. But again, "mescalin can never solve that problem; it can only pose it, apocalyptically, for those to whom it has never before presented itself."

Second, throughout *The Doors of Perception* Huxley keeps reminding us that poets, artists, visionaries (and he identifies them by name) have known all that he is talking about without the need of a stimulant, and suggesting that their experiences were far superior to those of the mescalin taker. Before he himself took the drug, his fervent hope was that it "would admit me, at least for a few hours, into the kind of inner world described by Blake and AE."

Apparently what Zaehner objected to was Huxley's non-Christian terminology, for one sees that Zaehner in *Mysticism Sacred and Profane* is attempting to make out a case for the superior merits of "Christian" mysticism as opposed to the mysticism of other religions. He gives a chapter each to most of them, and though he would accept that the mysticism of every religion is sacred, he believes that that of Christianity is the only true one and most sacred of them all. The fact remains that, barring a few unimportant external differences, all religious or mystical experiences are basically alike. Either they are all wrong or all equally right: the many paths to God. Fortunately, the mystics themselves reject a sectarian approach; none of them ever claimed an exclusive rank for his experiences or his method. The humility of Christ or the Buddha was so profound that they never set up separate orders in their names; their disciples did that. True mysticism is inherently nondenominational. It is a spiritual experience in which one transcends all party allegiances.

Huxley, in *The Doors of Perception,* is classifying his visions in accordance with this nonsectarian attitude. For him the ultimate reality is nameless and shapeless, and underlies every living object that we see or are confronted with—we being a part of the same reality. Before he took mescalin, he was aware of this identity only at the intellectual level. Afterwards he became aware of it more fully, his entire being participating in that awareness.

He is looking at a chair—"I spent several minutes —or was it several centuries?—not merely gazing at those bamboo legs, but actually *being* them—or rather being myself in them; or, to be still more accurate (for 'I' was not involved in the case, nor in a certain sense were 'they') being my Not-self in the Not-self which was the chair." Sentences like this puzzle Zaehner and he at once takes off after Huxley. Not that he does not understand Huxley's argument. But since his presentation does not conform to Zaehner's theistic conditioning, it irks him to accept it. So he digs up the dogmatic definition of "The Beatific Vision" (as "generally accepted" by the Christian Church) and questions Huxley for giving it a broader monistic meaning: "I had always understood that the Beatific Vision means a direct apperception of God, not through a glass, darkly, but face to face." Repeatedly Zaehner refers to Huxley's ideas as "confused," "incoherent" or "self-contradictory." But Emerson in *The Over-Soul* points out how confused and self-contradictory is the idea of immortality of the individual soul. "The moment the doctrine of the immortality is separately taught, man is already fallen," he records. Jesus never taught any such immortality; man as individual must die. He can continue to live only as a part of some universal spirit.

And that is what Huxley is doing, affirming the oneness of things—the primary concern of all mystics. To Zaehner the personality of an individual, his being, his "I," is very important. He cannot imagine a situation where that "I," that individual personality may be totally lost. The mystic, on the other hand, is constantly aiming at the extinction of the "I" so that it may be merged into the bigger "I" of the universe. At the final stage, the mystic has no separate existence. The experiencer is completely lost in the experience.

Either this is beyond Zaehner's comprehension or he is unwilling to accept the phenomenon. But for Huxley, all reality is finally one. By self, he means the small "I," the personality of each person or object. By Not-self, he means the common reality behind that person or object. While the selves in their external shapes and forms vary from person to person, from object to object, the reality that permeates them is identical. When Huxley calls this reality (in himself or the chair) Not-self, it is his way of coming to terms with it. Normally we capitalize the first letter of the word and call it Self, as distinguished from the small physical self of the individual. Huxley has many other names for it, however, in addition to Not-self. He calls it Eternity, Infinity, the Absolute, Suchness, Is-ness, the Great Spirit, Void, Mind at Large, Godhead, the Dharma-Body of the Buddha, Being-Awareness-Bliss, *Sat Chit Ananda*, The Beatific Vision, Inner Light, All is in All, Truth —all within the confines of this short book, *The Doors of Perception*. Emerson has yet another name for this great spirit, which has no shape and body; he calls it the Over-Soul. Sections of Emerson's highly challenging essay are included here, to show how a mystic never imagines a universe made up of small units. For the mystic what matters is not the individual selves but the Self.

In his observations on the mystic union, Huxley is therefore completely correct. Indeed, it may be taken as certain that most people who use a drug as an escape into a world of larger beauty do so not only in the hope of forgetting their present worries but also in order to identify themselves with something genuinely supreme.

But what Huxley does not see is that what actually happened to him under mescalin did not go far enough in its newness. This is the most essential aspect of a mystic vision—that it cannot be compared to anything known by man before, it is utterly orginal. Huxley draws the right inferences; but mystic visions are not a matter of inferences. In a book entitled *Language in Thought and Action* Professor S. Hayakawa defines inference as "a statement about the unknown made on the basis of the known." He is using "unknown" here as a synonym for unfamiliar things of the world. But the mystic Unknown, the Great Spirit or Over-Soul, can never be defined at all in the language of man. Words fail when one reaches that level.

Similarly, one notices that Huxley's images are derived only from things we already know, a chair, a pair of trousers, a tapestry, a painting, a book, a vase of flowers, etc. They are only a glorification of the known—the known seen in a different light, heightened perhaps, but nevertheless familiar.

In this context, it is doubtful if any drug can induce an experience which is not, in one form or the other, a mutation of the known. The philosopher

John Locke propounded the theory of *tabula rasa,* in which the human mind is conceived as a blank slate at birth; as the years go by, the slate becomes crowded with memories and impressions. And all the visions or ideas any man ever projects are only a variation of those impressions. Try explaining color to a congenitally blind man, Locke says. You cannot. The man has never known what color is and cannot visualize it from the account of another. This is equally true of the description of sound to a man deaf from birth. Freud attributed absolute values to dreams; but a man's dreams, too, are conditioned by what he has known or seen.

When the use of drugs spread, it was for a while imagined—and still is, by men like Timothy Leary, for instance—that they offered a new way from the known into the unknown. But all available record of experiences with drugs shows that the hallucinations, whether visual or auditory, almost always conform to a pattern, determined first by biological factors common to all and then by an individual's personal disposition. Heinrich Klüver in his excellent piece "Hallucinatory Constants" figures out these "constants" for us. And if we compare the five extracts included in Section II on Experiences with Klüver's reductions, these certainly seem to be valid.

As for the psychological freedom brought about by drugs, that too is a questionable hypothesis. Freedom from problems can only be achieved by dealing with them. A drug may knock you out or speed you up for an hour, two hours, or more, but the moment you are your normal self again you find those problems still looming before you. A Chinese proverb says that in order to walk a thousand miles, you must take the first step. By going high on a drug that first step into reality is avoided.

The passages in Section II on Experiences appear in order of writing. Fitz Hugh Ludlow, with whom the section opens, was the first American drug user to leave a considerable body of literature on the subject. Trained to be a lawyer, Ludlow instead devoted his life to literature and writing. A man of brilliant intellect, he died in Switzerland in 1870 at the age of thirty-four, his early death being attributed to the use of hashish. The extract included here is taken from *The Hasheesh Eater*, published by Harper & Brothers in 1857. His memoir is written in the fashion of De Quincey, but whereas De Quincey is very subjective, Ludlow throughout speaks of himself as an "Experimenter," a scientific investigator who records his reactions and those of his friends to hashish in detail.

Christopher Isherwood's "A Visit to Anselm Oakes" is fiction, but it reads as if based on actual experience. The protagonist is called Christopher Isherwood, and, as Isherwood himself tells us in his brief explanatory note, it offers "an adventure in hashish-taking."

Charles Baudelaire's "The Theatre of Seraphim" in Section III contains one of the few detailed accounts of a woman on drugs. But Baudelaire's confidante—whom he calls a "mature woman"—repeatedly tells us that after the drug she felt more captive than before. "The idea of confinement dominated my spirit," she records. Both these pieces are disturbing because Isherwood and Baudelaire concern them-

selves more with the face of evil than with that of
beauty. The Beatific Vision becomes beatific only in
its penultimate stage; before that it is a dual or mul-
tiple entity, comprising many shades of beauty and
many shades of evil. While most drug users recount
the horrors or phantoms that visited them in their
hallucinations, Isherwood and Baudelaire are out to
search for evil by design. Since life is so full of pain
and suffering, and since there are so many tempta-
tions that negate our good resolutions, they choose
to seek out evil deliberately. And the face of it they
turn up is frightening indeed. Many of us can go no
further than that—the baffling syndrome of stark
evil—and drugs only lead us into a worse quagmire.
Isherwood calls these hallucinations "the great
horrors"; and Baudelaire speaks of "their despotic
character," which weighs the spirit down. Both see
drugs as a form of withdrawal from life, not of participation in it.

The third passage in Section III, by William
Blair, is included to show the medical damage that
drugs can do. Blair, an Englishman, had mastered
six languages before he was thirteen—Greek, Latin,
Hebrew, Italian, Persian and English. He could find
no employment in England because of his drug habit
and came to the United States but could find no employment here either. Finally, in extreme poverty, he
was admitted to the City Hospital of New York for a
"cure" (the first case of a drug "cure" on record).
Blair deserted the hospital one night without informing the authorities. He was seen wandering the
streets of New York in an abject condition and it is

believed that he died there despite his great wish to return to England. His account, "An Opium-Eater in America," was written in the hospital in 1835, and published in 1842 in the magazine *The Knicker-bocker*. In some ways it is an amateurish narration, impetuous and overemotional. But of Blair's gifts, and the tragedy his opium habit brought him, there seems little doubt. Many accounts exist of people ruined by drugs, but few of such a potential genius coming to grief.

Little has been said so far of the medical dangers inherent in the use of drugs. Depending on how strong the constitution, one may go on taking them for years, but in the long run drugs do appear to ruin the system much earlier than old age or natural causes. Wide publicity as to these dangers should be the primary business of the Bureau of Narcotics. Cures with methadone and other means should be made easily available to all. Research should be pursued to produce a milder variety of marijuana or hashish for public use. This drug is supposedly the least hallucinogenic. If a mild form, medically safe, could be developed, society might accept it as it does tobacco and alcohol—as a means of social relaxation and pleasure. But the abuse of even a mild drug can be dangerous and morbidly confining.

The section entitled Limitations serves to establish that the experiences derived from drugs are invariably a repetition of the old. If it is a physical hallucination, we will find its parallel in Klüver's "constants." If it is a psychological feeling of uplift, Baudelaire has an answer to it: it is merely an exaggeration of what is already "dominant" in man's nature; "absolutely nothing but what is naturally excessive."

Only in genuine mysticism is the experience totally new. What one sees or hears here is full of bliss beyond words, of peace beyond human understanding. The equations of Locke and *tabula rasa* are finally discarded, for what ensues is not of man's making. It happens to him as part of a divine grace. He is absorbed into that total complex of creation where both the creation and the man rise to a new level.

But how can we combat the drift toward pseudo mysticism that the drug culture has set in motion? Only by a renewal of the true religious ends of life. We don't have much choice really, for all other remedies have been tried and found wanting. Religion may have served as opium for some, and in its proselytizing zeal may also have done disservice to the glory of God. But religion has also been the greatest single civilizing influence in the history of man. It taught him to have forbearance, to share his good fortune with others, to care for the suffering of another. In short, it taught him the virtues of self-denial, and in so doing raised him a step above the primitive beast he was before.

In the winter of 1947 and early 1948, in the last months of the life of Mahatma Gandhi, I was fortunate enough to have the privilege of listening to that great man every evening at his prayer meetings. Gandhi was then staying in New Delhi. As was his habit, he held a public prayer meeting every evening, at which texts from different religious scriptures were read and he answered questions of his audience.

At one of these meetings I asked him timidly if he were to set truth and nonviolence aside, what other message he would like to leave for humanity. It was a flippant question, to some extent asked in a spirit of defiance, since after the hundreds of thousands of people who had been massacred in the violence after partition, we youngsters were in no mood to listen to any doctrine of "truth and nonviolence." But Gandhi, as usual, took the question seriously, as though I were his equal. He looked at me for a while through his glasses, seemed to think inwardly, then nodded his head more to himself than to me, and answered with just a flicker of a smile that he could not set nonviolence and truth aside for a moment. But if he were to add another item of faith, he would say, "Live frugally." And he went on: "Since so much of mankind is in suffering, live as simply as you can."

The doctrine of self-denial all over again. Live in the awareness of the pain of your fellow man. A better concept than this humanity has not been able to posit, despite its many inventions and its conquests of nature and outer space.

The last section of this book, The Way Out, is intended in praise of the various religions that have served man over the centuries. Today we are no longer attracted by the decadent element in any religion. A blind devotion to personalities or adherence to ritual does not satisfy us. Hence here I have included two extracts that suggest an unorthodox approach to religion. The first of these is based on a

talk I had with Krishnamurti. The second is from
Emerson's "The Over-Soul," the meaning of which is
self-explanatory.

When in the winter of 1967 Maharishi Mahesh
Yogi visited New York, admission to his lecture in
Madison Square Garden was $10 a person mini-
mum. The thousands who flocked there and the
many more who were turned away again indicates
our pressing need for spiritual enlightenment. But
the Maharishi's method turned out to be no better
than another drug, and the disillusionment of many
was quick to follow. In my own restless wanderings,
I arrived in the Maharishi's ashram in the Himalayas
in July 1965. The Maharishi was not then on one of
his international tours and was gracious enough to
receive me at once. The first thing that struck me
was the lavishness of his establishment. Besides acres
of land and other buildings for his followers, there
was an ultra-modern bungalow exclusively for his
use atop a hill, with the Ganges flowing in the valley
below. The furnishings, the curtains, the rugs in the
bungalow were all expensive. The constant hum of
air conditioners reverberated in every room—that is
a luxury only the very rich can afford in India. I was
at once reminded of what Gandhi had said about living frugally, and the opulence of this ashram
seemed positively offensive.

But what finally made me lose interest in the Maharishi was when he said he could teach me to
control my mind and be at peace "in three days." In
his personal bearing the Maharishi was very gentle.
Nor was there any effort on his part to push me into
believing in him. But three days! It was as though

Christ had suffered on the Cross for nothing, the martyrs had died in the arena in vain—if the whole thing was as simple as that. When later I quoted this to Krishnamurti, he said: "Sir, I don't have to tell you—it's so juvenile!"

Krishnamurti would say the same of any other system of thought, including his own, if the teachings could be reduced to a simple code and practiced as such. He is the most daring religious thinker of the century; for the past forty years he has spoken ceaselessly against all religious authority and in favor of spiritual knowledge derived from self-analysis. Any quick absolutions or three-day meditations are for him only formulas of convenience that must perforce be rejected.

But there isn't so great a contradiction between religions of faith and religions of skepticism as might at first appear. An element of faith is implicit in Krishnamurti's doubt, otherwise he couldn't be talking of the unknown. Even the atheistic existentialists, who reject "essence" but accept "existence," have that much faith—a faith in existence, which if it does not proceed from essence is at least a part of *some* essence. And once we have freed established religions from the dogmas introduced into them, their message is again one of constant self-analysis. In *Katha Upanishad* it is written that the path to salvation is like "the sharp edge of a razor." The way of Christ and the way of the Buddha are no easier, if we read what they said carefully. Religions of faith emphasize a steadfast search for the glory of the inner self.

So a revival of religious awareness in life, whether

through a religion of doubt and skepticism or of faith, seems to me the only answer to the challenge of drugs. And, like the proverbial charity, such faith has to begin at home. The unit of spiritual reformation has to be not the church or the temple, but the family: parents who by personal example lead their children once again along the path to self-denial. At one stage we used to talk of virtues as sanctities. Now we should present them as imperatives.

J. W. Dunne in *An Experiment With Time* presents the riddle of a painter sketching a scene in which he wants to include the total reality of the present moment, himself included. So he paints a scene in which he shows a man painting the visual scene before him. But he soon realizes that a part of himself, the part which is actually doing the painting, is left out. So he paints another canvas, in which a man is painting another man painting a scene. But again a small fraction of the man actually doing the painting is left out. This results in a series of regressive pictures, but in each a minute part of the original painter continues to remain out of the artist's reach, the moral being that man cannot objectively conceive of a revelation of which he himself is a part. Hence any denial of God or a supreme force by a small section of that total reality appears not only pompous but irrational.

Once we have returned to religious enquiry, once we have reintroduced moral suffering by choice, once we have known the value of solitude, once the fears of the mind are exposed through self-knowledge and meditation, once we move with courage in the face of boredom, there comes an intoxication, a turning on, that no drug in the world can produce—the intoxication of being in tune with the rhythm of nature. Most of us can never rise above this level. But this intermediate stage itself would be infinitely superior to the disjointed and incoherent uplift produced by drugs. One walks in repose, in peace. It is a true and pure levitation—one walks a few inches above the ground. Colors and sounds take on a different tonality, the wind smells different. The individual exudes a perfume of well-being that is infectious. And rarely, very very rarely, if one is truly blessed, one passes into a further extension of being which is a moment of utter bliss, devoid of time and space.

Section II | *Experiences*

1. FITZ HUGH LUDLOW

The Hasheesh Eater

One morning, in the spring of 185–, I dropped in upon the doctor for my accustomed lounge.

"Have you seen," said he, "my new acquisitions?"

I looked toward the shelves in the direction of which he pointed, and saw, added since my last visit, a row of comely pasteboard cylinders inclosing vials of the various extracts prepared by Tilden & Co. Arranged in order according to their size, they confronted me, as pretty a little rank of medicinal sharpshooters as could gratify the eye of an amateur. I approached the shelves, that I might take them in review.

A rapid glance showed most of them to be old acquaintances. "Conium, taraxacum, rhubarb—ha! what is this? Cannabis Indica?" "That," answered the doctor, looking with a parental fondness upon his new treasure, "is a preparation of the East Indian hemp, a powerful agent in cases of lock-jaw." On the strength of this introduction, I took down the little archer, and, removing his outer verdant coat, began the further prosecution of his acquaintance. To pull out a broad and shallow cork was the work of an instant, and it revealed to me an olive-brown extract,

of the consistency of pitch, and a decided aromatic
odor. Drawing out a small portion upon the point of
my penknife, I was just going to put it to my tongue,
when "Hold on!" cried the doctor; "do you want to
kill yourself? That stuff is deadly poison." "Indeed!"
I replied; "no, I cannot say that I have any settled
determination of that kind"; and with that I replaced
the cork, and restored the extract, with all its appur-
tenances, to the shelf.

The remainder of my morning's visit in the sanc-
tum was spent in consulting the Dispensatory under
the title "Cannabis Indica." The sum of my discover-
ies there may be found, with much additional information, in that invaluable popular work, Johnston's
Chemistry of Common Life. This being universally
accessible, I will allude no further to the result of
that morning's researches than to mention the three
following conclusions to which I came.

First, the doctor was both right and wrong; right,
inasmuch as a sufficiently large dose of the drug, if it
could be retained in the stomach, would produce
death, like any other narcotic, and the ultimate effect
of its habitual use had always proved highly injurious to mind and body; wrong, since moderate
doses of it were never immediately deadly, and many
millions of people daily employed it as an indulgence
similarly to opium. Second, it was the hasheesh referred to by Eastern travelers, and the subject of a
most graphic chapter from the pen of Bayard Tay-
lor, which months before had moved me powerfully
to curiosity and admiration. Third, I would add it to
the list of my former experiments.

In pursuance of this last determination, I waited till my friend was out of sight, that I might not terrify him by that which he considered a suicidal venture, and then quietly uncapping my little archer a second time, removed from his store of offensive armor a pill sufficient to balance the ten grain weight of the sanctorial scales. This, upon the authority of Pereira and the Dispensatory, I swallowed without a tremor as to the danger of the result.

Making all due allowance for the fact that I had not taken my hasheesh bolus fasting, I ought to experience its effects within the next four hours. That time elapsed without bringing the shadow of a phenomenon. It was plain that my dose had been insufficient.

For the sake of observing the most conservative prudence, I suffered several days to go by without a repetition of the experiment, and then, keeping the matter equally secret, I administered to myself a pill of fifteen grains. This second was equally ineffectual with the first.

Gradually, by five grains at a time, I increased the dose to thirty grains, which I took one evening half an hour after tea. I had now almost come to the conclusion that I was absolutely unsusceptible of the hasheesh influence. Without any expectation that this last experiment would be more successful than the former ones, and indeed with no realization of the manner in which the drug affected those who did make the experiment successfully, I went to pass the evening at the house of an intimate friend. In music and conversation the time passed pleasantly. The clock struck ten, reminding me that three hours had elapsed since the dose was taken, and as yet not an unusual symptom had appeared. I was provoked to think that this trial was as fruitless as its predecessors.

Ha! what means this sudden thrill? A shock, as of some unimagined vital force, shoots without warning through my entire frame, leaping to my fingers, ends, piercing my brain, startling me till I almost spring from my chair.

I could not doubt it. I was in the power of the hasheesh influence. My first emotion was one of uncontrollable terror—a sense of getting something which I had not bargained for. That moment I would have given all I had or hoped to have to be as I was three hours before.

No pain anywhere—not a twinge in any fibre— yet a cloud of unutterable strangeness was settling upon me, and wrapping me impenetrably in from all that was natural or familiar. Endeared faces, well known to me of old, surrounded me, yet they were not with me in my loneliness. I had entered upon a tremendous life which they could not share. If the disembodied ever return to hover over the hearthstone which once had a seat for them, they look upon their friends as I then looked upon mine. A nearness of place, with an infinite distance of state, a connection which had no possible sympathies for the wants of that hour of revelation, an isolation none the less perfect for seeming companionship.

Still I spoke; a question was put to me, and I answered it; I even laughed at a bon mot. Yet it was not my voice which spoke; perhaps one which I once had far away in another time and another place. For a while I knew nothing that was going on externally, and then the remembrance of the last remark which had been made returned slowly and indistinctly, as some trait of a dream will return after many days, puzzling us to say where we have been conscious of it before.

A fitful wind all the evening had been sighing down the chimney; it now grew into the steady hum of a vast wheel in accelerating motion. For a while this hum seemed to resound through all space. I was stunned by it—I was absorbed in it. Slowly the revolution of the wheel came to a stop, and its monotonous din was changed for the reverberating peal of a grand cathedral organ. The ebb and flow of its inconceivably solemn tone filled me with a grief that was more than human. I sympathized with the dirge-like cadence as spirit sympathizes with spirit. And then, in the full conviction that all I heard and felt was real, I looked out of my isolation to see the effect of the music on my friends. Ah! we were in separate worlds indeed. Not a trace of appreciation on any face.

Perhaps I was acting strangely. Suddenly a pair of busy hands, which had been running neck and neck all the evening with a nimble little crochet-needle over a race-ground of pink and blue silk, stopped at their goal, and their owner looked at me steadfastly. Ah! I was found out—I had betrayed myself. In terror I waited, expecting every instant to hear the word "hasheesh." No, the lady only asked me some question connected with the previous conversation. As mechanically as an automaton I began to reply. As I heard once more the alien and unreal tones of my own voice, I became convinced that it was some one else who spoke, and in another world. I sat and listened; still the voice kept speaking. Now for the first time I experienced that vast change which hash-eesh makes in all measurements of time. The first word of the reply occupied a period sufficient for the action of a drama; the last left me in complete igno-rance of any point far enough back in the past to date the commencement of the sentence. Its enuncia-tion might have occupied years. I was not in the same life which had held me when I heard it begun.

And now, with time, space expanded also. At my friend's house one particular arm-chair was always reserved for me. I was sitting in it at a distance of hardly three feet from the centre-table around which the members of the family were grouped. Rapidly that distance widened. The whole atmosphere seemed ductile, and spun endlessly out into great spaces sur-rounding me on every side. We were in a vast hall, of which my friends and I occupied opposite ex-tremities. The ceiling and the walls ran upward with a gliding motion, as if vivified by a sudden force of resistless growth.

Oh! I could not bear it. I should soon be left alone in the midst of an infinity of space. And now more and more every moment increased the conviction that I was watched. I did not know then, as I learned afterward, that suspicion of all earthly things and persons was the characteristic of the hasheesh delirium.

In the midst of my complicated hallucination, I could perceive that I had a dual existence. One portion of me was whirled unresistingly along the track of this tremendous experience, the other sat looking down from a height upon its double, observing, reasoning, and serenely weighing all the phenomena. This calmer being suffered with the other by sympathy, but did not lose its self-possession. Presently it warned me that I must go home, lest the growing effect of the hasheesh should incite me to some act which might frighten my friends. I acknowledged the force of this remark very much as if it had been made by another person, and rose to take my leave. I advanced toward the centre-table. With every step its distance increased. I nerved myself as for a long pedestrian journey. Still the lights, the faces, the furniture receded. At last, almost unconsciously, I reached them. It would be tedious to attempt to convey the idea of the time which my leave-taking consumed, and the attempt, at least with all minds that have not passed through the same experience, would be as impossible as tedious. At last I was in the street.

Beyond me the view stretched endlessly away. It was an unconverging vista, whose nearest lamps seemed separated from me by leagues. I was doomed to pass through a merciless stretch of space. A soul just disenthralled, setting out for his flight beyond the farthest visible star, could not be more overwhelmed with his newly-acquired conception of the sublimity of distance than I was at that moment. Solemnly I began my infinite journey.

Before long I walked in entire unconsciousness of all around me. I dwelt in a marvelous inner world. I existed by turns in different places and various states of being. Now I swept my gondola through the moonlit lagoons of Venice. Now Alp on Alp towered above my view, and the glory of the coming sun flashed purple light upon the topmost icy pinnacle. Now in the primeval silence of some unexplored tropical forest I spread my feathery leaves, a giant fern, and swayed and nodded in the spice-gales over a river whose waves at once sent up clouds of music and perfume. My soul changed to a vegetable essence, thrilled with a strange and unimagined ecstasy. The palace of Al Haroun could not have brought me back to humanity.

I will not detail all the transmutations of that walk. Ever and anon I returned from my dreams into consciousness, as some well-known house seemed to leap out into my path, awaking me with a shock. The whole way homeward was a series of such awakings and relapses into abstraction and delirium until I reached the corner of the street in which I lived.

Here a new phenomenon manifested itself. I had just awaked for perhaps the twentieth time, and my eyes were wide open. I recognized all surrounding objects, and began calculating the distance home. Suddenly, out of a blank wall at my side a muffled figure stepped into the path before me. His hair, white as snow, hung in tangled elf-locks on his shoulders, where he carried also a heavy burden, like unto the well-filled sack of sins which Bunyan places on the back of his pilgrim. Not liking his manner, I stepped aside, intending to pass around him and go on my way. This change of our relative position allowed the blaze of a neighboring street-lamp to fall full on his face, which had hitherto been totally obscured. Horror unspeakable! I shall never, till the day I die, forget that face. Every lineament was stamped with the records of a life black with damning crime; it glared upon me with a ferocious wickedness and a stony despair which only he may feel who is entering on the retribution of the unpardonable sin. He might have sat to a demon painter as the ideal of Shelley's Cenci. I seemed to grow blasphemous in looking at him, and, in an agony of fear, began to run away. He detained me with a bony hand, which pierced my wrist like talons, and, slowly taking down the burden from his own shoulders, laid it upon mine. I threw it off and pushed him away. Silently he returned and restored the weight. Again I repulsed him, this time crying out, "Man, what do you mean?" In a voice which impressed me with the sense of wickedness as his face had done, he replied, "You *shall* bear my burden with me," and a third time laid it on my shoulders. For the last time I hurled it aside, and, with all my force, dashed him from me. He reeled backward and fell, and before he could recover his disadvantage I had put a long distance between us.

Through the excitement of my struggle with this

phantasm the effects of the hasheesh had increased mightily. I was bursting with an uncontrollable life; I strode with the thews of a giant. Hotter and faster came my breath; I seemed to pant like some tremendous engine. An electric energy whirled me resistlessly onward; I feared for myself lest it should burst its fleshly walls, and glance on, leaving a wrecked frame-work behind it.

At last I entered my own house. During my absence a family connection had arrived from abroad, and stood ready to receive my greeting. Partly restored to consciousness by the naturalness of home-faces and the powerful light of a chandelier which shed its blaze through the room, I saw the necessity of vigilance against betraying my condition, and with an intense effort suppressing all I felt, I approached my friend, and said all that is usual on such occasions. Yet recent as I was from my conflict with the supernatural, I cast a stealthy look about me, that I might learn from the faces of the others if, after all, I was shaking hands with a phantom, and making inquiries about the health of a family of hallucinations. Growing assured as I perceived no symptoms of astonishment, I finished the salutation and sat down.

It soon required all my resolution to keep the secret which I had determined to hold inviolable. My sensations began to be terrific—not from any pain that I felt, but from the tremendous mystery of all around me and within me. By an appalling introversion, all the operations of vitality which, in our ordinary state, go on unconsciously, came vividly into my experience. Through every thinnest corporeal tis-

sue and minutest vein I could trace the circulation of
the blood along each inch of its progress. I knew
when every valve opened and when it shut; every
sense was preternaturally awakened; the room was
full of a great glory. The beating of my heart was so
clearly audible that I wondered to find it unnoticed
by those who were sitting by my side. Lo, now, that
heart became a great fountain, whose jet played upward with loud vibrations, and, striking upon the
roof of my skull as on a gigantic dome, fell back with
a splash and echo into its reservoir. Faster and faster
came the pulsations, until at last I heard them no
more, and the stream became one continuously
pouring flood, whose roar resounded through all my
frame. I gave myself up for lost, since judgment,
which still sat unimpaired above my perverted
senses, argued that congestion must take place in a
few moments, and close the drama with my death.
But my clutch would not yet relax from hope. The
thought struck me, Might not this rapidity of circulation be, after all, imaginary? I determined to find
out.

Going to my own room, I took out my watch, and
placed my hand upon my heart. The very effort
which I made to ascertain the reality gradually
brought perception back to its natural state. In the
intensity of my observations, I began to perceive that
the circulation was not as rapid as I had thought.
From a pulseless flow it gradually came to be apprehended as a hurrying succession of intense throbs,
then less swift and less intense, till finally, on com-
paring it with the second-hand, I found that about

90 a minute was its average rapidity. Greatly comforted, I desisted from the experiment. Almost instantly the hallucination returned. Again I dreaded apoplexy, congestion, hemorrhage, a multiplicity of nameless deaths, and drew my picture as I might be found on the morrow, stark and cold, by those whose agony would be redoubled by the mystery of my end. I reasoned with myself; I bathed my forehead—it did no good. There was one resource left: I would go to a physician.

With this resolve, I left my room and went to the head of the staircase. The family had all retired for the night, and the gas was turned off from the burner in the hall below. I looked down the stairs: the depth was fathomless; it was a journey of years to reach the bottom! The dim light of the sky shone through the narrow panes at the sides of the front door, and seemed a demon-lamp in the middle darkness of the abyss. I never could get down! I sat me down despairingly upon the topmost step.

Suddenly a sublime thought possessed me. If the distance be infinite, I am immortal. It shall be tried. I commenced the descent, wearily, wearily down through my league-long, year-long journey. To record my impressions in that journey would be to repeat what I have said of the time of hasheesh. Now stopping to rest as a traveler would turn aside at a wayside inn, now toiling down through the lonely darkness, I came by-and-by to the end, and passed out into the street.

On reaching the porch of the physician's house, I

rang the bell, but immediately forgot whom to ask for. No wonder; I was on the steps of a palace in Milan—no (and I laughed at myself for the blunder), I was on the staircase of the Tower of London. So I should not be puzzled through my ignorance of Italian. But whom to ask for? This question recalled me to the real bearings of the place, but did not suggest its requisite answer. Whom shall I ask for? I began setting the most cunning traps of hypothesis to catch the solution of the difficulty. I looked at the surrounding houses; of whom had I been accustomed to think as living next door to them? This did not bring it. Whose daughter had I seen going to school from this house but the very day before? Her name was Julia—Julia—and I thought of every combination which had been made with this name from Julia Domna down to Giulia Grisi. Ah! now I had it —Julia H.; and her father naturally bore the same name. During this intellectual rummage I had rung the bell half a dozen times, under the impression that I was kept waiting a small eternity. When the servant opened the door she panted as if she had run for her life. I was shown up stairs to Dr. H.'s room, where he had thrown himself down to rest after a tedious operation. Locking the door after me with an air of determined secrecy, which must have conveyed to him pleasant little suggestions of a design upon his life, I approached his bedside.

"I am about to reveal to you," I commenced, "something which I would not for my life allow to come to other ears. Do you pledge me your eternal silence?"

"I do; what is the matter?"

"I have been taking hasheesh—Cannabis Indica, and I fear that I am going to die."

"How much did you take?"

"Thirty grains."

"Let me feel your pulse." He placed his finger on my wrist and counted slowly, while I stood waiting to hear my death-warrant. "Very regular," shortly spoke the doctor; "triflingly accelerated. Do you feel any pain?" "None at all." "Nothing the matter with you; go home and go to bed." "But—is there—is there—no danger of—apoplexy?" "Bah!" said the doctor; and, having delivered himself of this opinion of my case, he lay down again. My hand was on the knob, when he stopped me with, "Wait a minute; I'll give you a powder to carry with you, and if you get frightened again after you leave me, you can take it as a sedative. Step out on the landing, if you please, and call my servant."

I did so, and my voice seemed to reverberate like thunder from every recess in the whole building. I was terrified at the noise I had made. I learned in after days that this impression is only one of the many due to the intense susceptibility of the sensorium as produced by hasheesh. At one time, having asked a friend to check me if I talked loudly or immoderately while in a state of fantasia among persons from whom I wished to conceal my state, I caught myself shouting and singing from very ecstasy, and reproached him with a neglect of his friendly office. I could not believe him when he assured me that I had not uttered an audible word.

The intensity of the inward emotion had affected the external through the internal ear.

I returned and stood at the foot of the doctor's bed. All was perfect silence in the room, and had been perfect darkness also but for the small lamp which I held in my hand to light the preparation of the powder when it should come. And now a still sublimer mystery began to enwrap me. I stood in a remote chamber at the top of a colossal building, and the whole fabric beneath me was steadily growing into the air. Higher than the topmost pinnacle of Bel's Babylonish temple—higher than Ararat—on, on forever into the lonely dome of God's infinite universe we towered ceaselessly. The years flew on; I heard the musical rush of their wings in the abyss outside of me, and from cycle to cycle, from life to life I careered, a mote in eternity and space. Suddenly emerging from the orbit of my transmigrations, I was again at the foot of the doctor's bed, and thrilled with wonder to find that we were both unchanged by the measureless lapse of time. The servant had not come.

"Shall I call her again?" "Why, you have this moment called her." "Doctor," I replied solemnly, and in language that would have seemed bombastic enough to any one who did not realize what I felt, "I will not believe you are deceiving me, but to me it appears as if sufficient time has elapsed since then for all the Pyramids to have crumbled back to dust." "Ha! ha! you are very funny to-night," said the doctor; "but here she comes, and I will send her for something which will comfort you on that score, and reestablish the Pyramids in your confidence." He gave the girl his orders, and she went out again.

The thought struck me that I would compare *my time* with other people's. I looked at my watch, found that its minute-hand stood at the quarter mark past eleven, and, returning it to my pocket, abandoned myself to my reflections.

Presently I saw myself a gnome imprisoned by a most weird enchanter, whose part I assigned to the doctor before me, in the Domdaniel caverns, "under the roots of the ocean." Here, until the dissolution of all things, was I doomed to hold the lamp that lit that abysmal darkness, while my heart, like a giant clock, ticked solemnly the remaining years of time. Now, this hallucination departing, I heard in the solitude of the night outside the sound of a wondrous heaving sea. Its waves, in sublime cadence, rolled forward till they met the foundations of the building; they smote them with a might which made the very topstone quiver, and then fell back, with hiss and hollow murmur, into the broad bosom whence they had arisen. Now through the street, with measured tread, an armed host passed by. The heavy beat of their footfall and the grinding of their brazen corslet-rings alone broke the silence, for among them all there was no more speech nor music than in a battalion of the dead. It was the army of the ages going by into eternity. A godlike sublimity swallowed up my soul. I was overwhelmed in a fathomless barathrum of time, but I leaned on God, and was immortal through all changes.

And now, in another life, I remembered that far

back in the cycles I had looked at my watch to measure the time through which I passed. The impulse
seized me to look again. The minute-hand stood half
way between fifteen and sixteen minutes past eleven.
The watch must have stopped; I held it to my ear;
no, it was still going. I had traveled through all
that immeasurable chain of dreams in thirty seconds. "My God!" I cried, "I am in eternity." In the
presence of that first sublime revelation of the soul's
own time, and her capacity for an infinite life, I
stood trembling with breathless awe. Till I die, that
moment of unveiling will stand in clear relief from
all the rest of my existence. I hold it still in unimpaired remembrance as one of the unutterable sanctities of my being. The years of all my earthly life to
come can never be as long as those thirty seconds.

Finally the servant reappeared. I received my
powder and went home. There was a light in one of
the upper windows, and I hailed it with unspeakable
joy, for it relieved me from a fear which I could not
conquer, that while I had been gone all familiar
things had passed away from earth. I was hardly safe
in my room before I doubted having ever been out of
it. "I have experienced some wonderful dream," said
I, "as I lay here after coming from the parlor." If I
had not been out, I reasoned that I would have no
powder in my pocket. The powder was there, and it
steadied me a little to find that I was not utterly hallucinated on every point. Leaving the light burning,
I set out to travel to my bed, which gently invited me
in the distance. Reaching it after a sufficient walk, I
threw myself down.

The judgment that must be passed upon the hasheesh life in retrospect is widely different from the
one which I formed during its progress. Now the
drug, with all its revelation of interior mysteries, its
glimpses of supernatural beauty and sublimity, appears as the very witch-plant of hell, the weed of
madness. At the time of its daily use, I forgave it for
all its pangs, for its cruel exercise of authority, its
resistless fascination, and its usurpation of the place
of all other excitement, at the intercession of the divine forms which it created for my soul, and which,
though growing rarer and rarer, when they were
present retained their glory until the last. Moreover,
through many ecstasies and many pains, I still supposed that I was only making experiments, and that,
too, in the most wonderful field of mind which could
be opened for investigation, and with an agent so de-
luding in its influence that the soul only became
aware that the strength of a giant was needed to escape when its locks were shorn.

In accordance with these facts, I did not suppose
that I was imperiling any friend of mine by giving
him an opportunity to make the same experiment
which he beheld producing in me phenomena so astonishing to a mind in love with research. Several of
my intimate associates applied to me for the means
of experimentally gratifying their curiosity upon the
subject, and to some of them, as favorable opportuni-
ties presented themselves, I administered hasheesh, remaining by their side during the progress of the
effects. In no other experience can difference of
temperament, physical and mental, produce such vari-

eties of phenomena; nowhere can we attain so well
defined an idea of this difference. I shall, therefore,
devote this chapter to the relation of some of the
more remarkable of these cases.

Upon William N—— hasheesh produced none of
the effects characteristic of fantasia. There was no
hallucination, no volitancy of unusual images before
the eye when closed. Circulation, however, grew to a
surprising fullness and rapidity, accompanied by the
same introversion of faculties and clear perception of
all physical processes which startled me in my
first experiment upon myself. There was stertorous
breathing, dilation of the pupil, and a drooping appearance of the eyelid, followed at last by a
comatose state, lasting for hours, out of which it was
almost impossible fully to arouse the energies. These
symptoms, together with a peculiar rigidity of the
muscular system, and inability to measure the precise compass and volume of the voice when speaking, brought the case nearer in resemblance to those
recorded by Dr. O'Shaughnessy, of Calcutta, as occurring under his immediate inspection among the
natives of India than any I have ever witnessed.

In William N—— I observed, however, one phenomenon which characterizes hasheesh existence in
persons of far different constitutions—the expansion
of time and space. Walking with him a distance not
exceeding a furlong, I have seen him grow weary and
assume a look of hopelessness, which he explained
by telling me that he never could traverse the immensity before him. Frequently, also, do I remember
his asking to know the time thrice in as many min-

utes, and when answered, he exclaimed, "Is it possible? I supposed it an hour since I last inquired." His temperament was a mixture of the phlegmatic and nervous, and he was generally rather unsusceptible to stimulus. I was anxious at the time that he should be favorably affected, since he had been, and afterward was still more so, in an eminent degree, the kindhearted assuager of my sufferings and increaser of my joys in many an experience of hasheesh. To him I ran, many a time, for companionship in my hasheesh journeyings, and always found in him full appreciation and sympathy.

I am now glad that he learned none of the fascination of the drug, for Heaven only, and not the hasheesh-eater in any wise, knows where it will lead him.

One of my friends in college was a man to whom it would have been physically, spiritually, and morally impossible ever to have borne any other name than Bob, the name by which he was called among all his intimates, and which has an air eminently expressive of his nature. Impulsive, enthusiastic in his affections, generous to a fault; excitable, fond of queer researches and romantic ventures, there is no other cognomen which would so typify him as to give more than a shadowy image of his constitution——none which would so incarnate him as not to leave some elbow of his inner being sticking out in the improper place. It is not surprising that a person of his temperament found much in the hasheesh condition that was strikingly attractive.

At half past seven in the evening, and consequently after supping instead of before, as I should have preferred, he took twenty-five grains of the drug. . . .

From the untoward lateness of the hour at which the dose was administered, it was half past ten o'clock before any effects began to show themselves in this case. At that time Bob, and Edward, the reading man, to whose favorable notice I had presented myself under the guise of a hippopotamus, were both seated, together with myself, in a well-lighted room, conversing. Suddenly Bob leaped up from the lounge on which he had been lying, and, with loud peals of laughter, danced wildly over the room. A strange light was in his eyes, and he gesticulated furiously, like a player in pantomime. I was not in the least surprised by these symptoms, for I realized precisely the state of mind through which he was passing; yet my other companion was astonished even to terror with the idea that the experimenter would permanently lose his sanity. Suddenly he stopped dancing, and trembling, as with an undefinable fear, he whispered, "What will become of me?" This question distinctly recalled all the horrible apprehensions of my first experiment; and, though satisfied of the perfect harmlessness of the result, I saw the necessity of steadying the sufferer's mind upon my own firm assurance of his safety, for the sake of giving him quiet and endurance. I replied, "Trust me, however singularly you may feel, you have not the slightest cause for fear. I have been where you are now, and, upon my

honor, guarantee you an unharmed return. No evil
will result to you; abandon yourself to the full force
of your feelings with perfect confidence that you are
in no danger." Entirely new and unconceived as is
the hasheesh-world, viewed for the first time, the man
of greatest natural courage is no more capable of
bearing its tremendous realities, unbraced by some
such exterior support, than the most feeble woman.

The delirium, now rapidly mounting to its height,
made it better that Bob should exert the supernatural
activity with which he was endued out of doors,
where the air was freer and less constraint was necessary. Clothing my words in as imaginative a garb
as I was master of, I therefore proposed to him that
we should set out on a journey through the wonderful lands of vision. We were soon upon the pavement, he leaping in unbounded delight at the prospect of the grand scenery to come, I ready to humor
to the utmost any pleasing fantasy which might possess him; and in the absence of such, or the presence
of the contrary, to suggest fine avenues for his
thought to follow up.

It will of course be perceived that I labor under a
great disadvantage from being compelled to relate
the progress of subjective states from an objective
point of view. My authority for all that I shall give in
this case will be my own observation of outward
phenomena and my friend's statement of interior ones,
which he gave to me upon returning to consciousness. . . .

On our first leaving the steps of the building, a

grand mosque rose upon his vision in the distance, its minarets flaunting with innumerable crescent-emblazoned flags. A mighty plain, covered with no other than a stinted grass, stretched between him and the mosque. Mounted upon Arab horses, with incredible swiftness we sped side by side toward the structure; and I knew when this imagination took place by the answers which he returned me upon my inquiry into the reasons of his prancing as we went. Before we reached the walls, arch and minaret had vanished, and, metamorphosed into an ostrich, he scoured the desert reaches, now utterly void of any human sign. Of this fact also I became aware at the moment from his own lips; for, although in perfect hallucination, the dual existence, as in me, was still capable of expressing its own states. . . . The night was much darker than it should have been for a hasheesh-eater's walk, who, it will be remembered, calls imperatively for light to tinge his visions. The hallucination of the ostrich still remaining, we passed out into the street through the stone gateway at the end of the college terrace. The sky above us was obscured by clouds, but the moon, now at her full, was about three breadths of her disk above the western horizon. I pointed through the trees to her radiant shield, and called Bob's attention to the peculiar beauty of the view. He clapped his hands in ecstasy, exclaiming, "Behold the eternal kingdom of the moonlight!" From that moment until the planet set, in this kingdom he walked. A silvery deliciousness transfused all things to his sight; his emotions rose and fell like tides with the thrill of the lunar influence. All that in past imaginings he had ever enjoyed of moonlit river views, terraces, castles, and slumberous gardens, was melted into this one vision of rapture.

At length the moon sank out of sight, and a thick darkness enveloped us in the lonely street, only relieved by the corner lamps, which dotted the long and drear prospective. For a while we walked silently. Presently I felt my companion shudder as he leaned upon my arm. "What is the matter, Bob?" I asked. "Oh! I am in unbearable horror," he replied. "If you can, save me!" "How do you suffer?" "This shower of soot which falls on me from heaven is dreadful!"

I sought to turn the current of his thoughts into another channel, but he had arrived at that place in his experience where suggestion is powerless. His world of the Real could not be changed by any inflow from ours of the Shadowy. I reached the same place in after days, and it was then as impossible for any human being to alter the condition which enwrapped me as it would have been for a brother on earth to stretch out his hands and rescue a brother writhing in the pangs of immortality. There are men in Oriental countries who make it their business to attend hasheesh-eaters during the fantasia, and profess to be able to lead them constantly in pleasant paths of hallucination. If indeed they possess this power, the delirium which they control must be a far more ductile state than any I have witnessed occurring under the influence of hasheesh at its height. In the present instance I found all suggestion powerless. The inner actuality of the visions and the terror of external darkness both defeated me.

Again, for a short distance, we went without speaking. And now my friend broke forth into a faint, yet bitter cry of "Pray for me! I shall be lost!" Though still knowing that he was in no ultimate danger, I felt that it was vain to tell him so, and, granting his request, ejaculated, "Oh best and wisest God, give peace unto this man!" "Stop! stop!" spoke my friend; "that name is terrible to me; I can not hear it. I am dying; take me instantly to a physician."

Aware that, though no such physical need existed, there was still a great spiritual one if I would make him calm, I immediately promised him that I would do as he asked, and directed our course to the nearest doctor. Now, demoniac shapes clutched at him from the darkness, cloaked from head to foot in inky palls, yet glaring with fiery eyes from the depths of their cowls. I felt him struggling, and by main force dragged him from their visionary hands. The place wherein he seemed to himself to be walking was a vast arena, encircled by tremendous walls. As from the bottom of a black barathrum, he looked up and saw the stars infinitely removed; they gazed mournfully at him with a human aspect of despairing pity, and he heard them faintly bewailing his perdition. Sulphurous fires rolled in the distance, upbearing on their waves agonized forms and faces of mockery, and demon watch-fires flared up fitfully on the impenetrable battlements around him. He did not speak a word, but I heard him groan with a tone that was full of fearful meaning. . . .

The next case which I shall mention is that of my friend Fred W——. His most wonderful experience —wonderful for its exceeding beauty, but still more so for the glimpse which it gave him of the mind's power of sympathetic perception—was a vision which he [once] had. Having taken hasheesh and felt its influence already for several hours, he still retained enough of conscious self-control to visit the room of a certain excellent pianist without exciting the suspicion of the latter. Fred threw himself upon a sofa immediately on entering, and asked the artist to play him some piece of music, without naming any one in particular.

The prelude began. With its first harmonious rise and fall the dreamer was lifted into the choir of a grand cathedral. Thenceforward it was heard no longer as exterior, but I shall proceed to tell how it was internally embodied in one of the most wonderful imaginative representations that it has ever been my lot to know.

The windows of nave and transept were emblazoned, in the most gorgeous coloring, with incidents culled from saintly lives. Far off in the chancel, monks were loading the air with essences that streamed from their golden censers; on the pavement, of inimitable mosaic, kneeled a host of reverent worshipers in silent prayer.

Suddenly, behind him, the great organ began a plaintive minor like the murmur of some bard reliev-

ing his heart in threnody. This minor was joined by
a gentle treble voice among the choir in which he
stood. The low wail rose and fell as with the expression of wholly human emotion. One by one the remaining singers joined in it, and now he heard, thrill-
ing to the very roof of the cathedral, a wondrous
miserere. But the pathetic delight of hearing was
soon supplanted by, or rather mingled with, a new
sight in the body of the pile below him. At the farther end of the nave a great door slowly swung open
and a bier entered, supported by solemn bearers.
Upon it lay a coffin covered by a heavy pall, which,
being removed as the bier was set down in the chancel, discovered the face of the sleeper. It was the dead
Mendelssohn!

The last cadence of the death-chant died away;
the bearers, with heavy tread, carried the coffin
through an iron door to its place in the vault; one by
one the crowd passed out of the cathedral, and at
last, in the choir, the dreamer stood alone. He turned
himself also to depart, and, awakened to complete
consciousness, beheld the pianist just resting
from the keys. "What piece have you been playing?"
asked Fred. The musician replied it was "Mendelssohn's Funeral March!"

This piece, Fred solemnly assured me, he had
never heard before. The phenomenon thus appears
inexplicable by any hypothesis which would regard it
as a mere coincidence. Whether this vision was suggested by an unconscious recognition of Mendelssohn's style in the piece performed, or, by the awaking of some unknown intuitional faculty, it was

produced as an original creation, I know not, but certainly it is as remarkable an instance of sympathetic clairvoyance as I ever knew.

Dan, the partner of my hasheesh-walk . . . in the town of P——, was, at the same time as myself, a member of the college. The Coryphæus of witty circles, and the light of all our festivals, he was still imaginative in higher spheres, and as worthily held the rostrum and the bard's chair as his place by the genial fireside or generous table. A poet, and an enthusiastic lover as well as performer of music, I supposed that the effect of hasheesh upon his susceptible temperament would be delightful in the extreme. But to such a result, the time at which he took the drug was one of the most unfavorable in the world—when his nervous system was in a state of even morbid excitability. We had started together on a walk when the thrill came on. And such a thrill—or, rather, such a succession of thrills—it is wonderful how a human organism could sustain. At first a cloud of impenetrable mystery inwrapt him; then upon the crown of his head a weight began to press. It increased in gravity without gaining bulk, and at last, breaking through the barrier of the skull, it slid down the spinal column like lightning, convulsing every nerve with one simultaneous shudder of agony.

This sensation was repeated again and again, until, with horror, he called on me to return, as assured as I had ever been in my first experiments that death was soon to be the result of the shock. I instantly obeyed his wish, and on reaching his room he lay down. Of a sudden all space expanded marvelously, and into the broad area where he reclined marched a multitude of bands from all directions, discoursing music upon all sorts of instruments, and each band playing a different march on a different key, yet all, by some scientific arrangement, preserving perfect harmony with each other, and most exquisitely keeping time. As the symphony increased in volume, so also did it heighten in pitch, until at last the needle-points of sound seemed to concenter in a demon music-box of incredible upper register, which whirled the apex of its scream through the dome of his head, inside of which it was playing.

Now, on the wall of the room, removed to a great distance by the hasheesh expansion, a monstrous head was spiked up, which commenced a succession of grimaces of the most startling yet ludicrous character. First its ferociously bearded under jaw extended forward indefinitely, and then, the jaw shooting back, the mouth opened from ear to ear. Now the nose spun out into absurd enormity, and now the eyes winked with the rapidity of lightning.

Yet suffering in Dan bore an excessive over-ratio to mirth. In his greatest pain he had framed a withering curse against some one who had entered the room, but when he tried to give it utterance his lips failed in their office as if paralyzed. I gave him water when his thirst had become extreme, and the . . . sensations of a cataract plunging down his throat which I have before described occurred so powerfully that he set the glass down, unwilling to risk the consequences of his draught.

Returning to consciousness, he did not, however, recover from the more moderate hasheesh effects for months. The nervous thrills which I have related reappeared to him at intervals, and his dreams constantly wore a hasheesh tint. Indeed, in all cases which I have known, this drug has retained a more enduring influence than any stimulant in the whole catalogue.

A number of experiments made upon other persons with more or less success, yet none of them characterized by any phenomena differing from those already detailed, prove conclusively that upon persons of the highest nervous and sanguine temperaments hasheesh has the strongest effect; on those of the bilious occasionally almost as powerful a one; while lymphatic constitutions are scarcely influenced at all except in some physical manner, such as vertigo, nausea, coma, or muscular rigidity. Yet to this statement there are striking exceptions, arising out of the operation of some latent forces of vitality which we have not yet included in our physical or psychical science. Until the laws which govern these are fully apprehended, hasheesh must ever remain a mystery, and its operation in any specific case an uncertainty.

2. HAVELOCK ELLIS

Mescal: A New Paradise

It has been known for some years that the Kiowa Indians of New Mexico are accustomed to eat, in their religious ceremonies, a certain cactus called Anhalonium Lewinii, or mescal button. Mescal—which must not be confounded with the intoxicating drink of the same name made from an agave—is found in the Mexican Valley of the Rio Grande, the ancestral home of the Kiowa Indians, as well as in Texas, and is a brown and brittle substance, nauseous and bitter to the taste, composed mainly of the blunt dried leaves of the plant. Yet, as we shall see, it has every claim to rank with haschisch and the other famous drugs which have procured for men the joys of an artificial paradise. Upon the Kiowa Indians, who first discovered its rare and potent virtues, it has had so strong a fascination that the missionaries among these Indians, finding here a rival to Christianity not yielding to moral suasion, have appealed to the secular arm, and the buying and selling of the drug has been prohibited by Government under severe penalties. Yet the use of mescal prevails among the Kiowas to this day.

It has indeed spread, and the mescal rite may be

said to be to-day the chief religion of all the tribes of the southern plains of the United States. The rite usually takes place on Saturday night; the men then sit in a circle within the tent round a large camp fire, which is kept burning brightly all the time. After prayer the leader hands each man four buttons, which are slowly chewed and swallowed, and altogether about ten or twelve buttons are consumed by each man between sundown and daybreak. Throughout the night the men sit quietly round the fire in a state of reverie—amid continual singing and the beating of drums by attendants—absorbed in the color visions and other manifestations of mescal intoxication, and about noon on the following day, when the effects have passed off, they get up and go about their business, without any depression or other unpleasant aftereffect.

There are five or six allied species of cacti which the Indians also use and treat with great reverence. Thus Mr. Carl Lumholtz has found that the Tarahumari, a tribe of Mexican Indians, worship various cacti as gods, only to be approached with uncovered heads. When they wish to obtain these cacti, the Tarahumari cense themselves with copal incense, and with profound respect dig up the god, careful lest they should hurt him, while women and children are warned from the spot. Even Christian Indians regard Hikori, the cactus god, as coequal with their own divinity, and make the sign of the cross in its presence. At all great festivals Hikori is made into a drink and consumed by the medicine man, or certain selected Indians, who sing as they partake of it, invoking Hikori to grant a "beautiful intoxication"; at the same time a rasping noise is made with sticks, and men and women dance a fantastic and picturesque dance —the women by themselves in white petticoats and tunics—before those who are under the influence of the god.

In 1891 Mr. James Mooney, of the United States Bureau of Ethnology, having frequently observed the mescal rites of the Kiowa Indians and assisted at them, called the attention of the Anthropological Society at Washington to the subject, and three years later he brought to Washington a supply of mescal, which was handed over for examination to Drs. Prentiss and Morgan. These investigators experimented on several young men, and demonstrated, for the first time, the precise character of mescal intoxication and the remarkable visions to which it gives rise. A little later Dr. Weir Mitchell, who, in addition to his eminence as a physician, is a man of marked æsthetic temperament, experimented on himself, and published a very interesting record of the brilliant visions by which he was visited under the influence of the plant. In the spring of the past year I was able to obtain a small sample of mescal in London, and as my first experiment with mescal was also, apparently, the first attempt to investigate its vision-producing properties outside America,[1]   will

---

[1] Lewin, of Berlin, indeed, experimented with Anhalonium Lewinii, to which he gave its name, as early as 1888, and as he found that even a small portion produced dangerous symptoms, he classed it amongst the extremely poisonous drugs, like strychnia. He failed to discover its vision-pro-

describe it in some detail, in preference to drawing on the previously published descriptions of the American observers.

On Good Friday I found myself entirely alone in the quiet rooms in the Temple which I occupy when in London, and judged the occasion a fitting one for a personal experiment. I made a decoction (a different method from that adopted in America) of three buttons, the full physiological dose, and drank this at intervals between 2:30 and 4:30 p. m. The first symptom observed during the afternoon was a certain consciousness of energy and intellectual power. This passed off, and about an hour after the final dose I felt faint and unsteady; the pulse was low, and I found it pleasanter to lie down. I was still able to read, and I noticed that a pale violet shadow floated over the page around the point at which my eyes were fixed. I had already noticed that objects not in the direct line of vision, such as my hands holding the book, showed a tendency to look obtrusive, heightened in color, almost monstrous, while, on closing my eyes, afterimages were vivid and prolonged. The appearance of visions with closed eyes was very gradual. At first there was merely a vague play of light and shade which suggested pictures, but never made them. Then the pictures became more definite, but too confused and crowded to be described, beyond saying that they were of the same character as the images of the kaleidoscope, symmet-

---

ducing properties, and it seems, in fact, highly probable that he was really experimenting with a different cactus from that now known by the same name.

rical groupings of spiked objects. Then, in the course
of the evening, they became distinct, but still indescribable—mostly a vast field of golden jewels, studded with red and green stones, ever changing. This
moment was, perhaps, the most delightful of the
experience, for at the same time the air around me
seemed to be flushed with vague perfume—producing with the visions a delicious effect—and all dis-
comfort had vanished, except a slight faintness and
tremor of the hands, which, later on, made it almost
impossible to guide a pen as I made notes of the experiment; it was, however, with an effort, always
possible to write with a pencil. The visions never
resembled familiar objects; they were extremely
definite, but yet always novel; they were constantly
approaching, and yet constantly eluding, the sem-
blance of known things. I would see thick, glorious
fields of jewels, solitary or clustered, sometimes brilliant and sparkling, sometimes with a dull rich glow.
Then they would spring up into flower-like shapes
beneath my gaze, and then seem to turn into gorgeous butterfly forms or endless folds of glistening,
iridescent, fibrous wings of wonderful insects; while
sometimes I seemed to be gazing into a vast hollow revolving vessel, on whose polished concave
mother-of-pearl surface the hues were swiftly changing. I was surprised, not only by the enormous
profusion of the imagery presented to my gaze, but
still more by its variety. Perpetually some totally new
kind of effect would appear in the field of vision;
sometimes there was swift movement, sometimes
dull, somber richness of color, sometimes glitter and

sparkle, once a startling rain of gold, which seemed
to approach me. Most usually there was a combination of rich, sober color, with jewel-like points of
brilliant hue. Every color and tone conceivable to me
appeared at some time or another. Sometimes all the
different varieties of one color, as of red, with scar-
lets, crimsons, pinks, would spring up together, or in
quick succession. But in spite of this immense profusion, there was always a certain parsimony and
æsthetic value in the colors presented. They were
usually associated with form, and never appeared in
large masses, or if so, the tone was very delicate. I
was further impressed, not only by the brilliance,
delicacy, and variety of the colors, but even more by
their lovely and various textures—fibrous, woven,
polished, glowing, dull, veined, semi-transparent—
the glowing effects, as of jewels, and the fibrous, as
of insects' wings, being perhaps the most prevalent.
Although the effects were novel, it frequently happened, as I have already mentioned, that they
vaguely recalled known objects. Thus, once the
objects presented to me seemed to be made of
exquisite porcelain, again they were like elaborate
sweetmeats, again of a somewhat Maori style of architecture; and the background of the pictures frequently recalled, both in form and tone, the delicate
architectural effects as of lace carved in wood, which
we associate with the mouchrabieh work of Cairo.
But always the visions grew and changed without
any reference to the characteristics of those real
objects of which they vaguely reminded me, and
when I tried to influence their course it was with

very little success. On the whole, I should say that
the images were most usually what might be called
living arabesques. There was often a certain incomplete tendency to symmetry, as though the underlying mechanism was associated with a large
number of polished facets. The same image was in
this way frequently repeated over a large part of the
field; but this refers more to form than to color, in
respect to which there would still be all sorts of delightful varieties, so that if, with a certain uniformity,
jewel-like flowers were springing up and expanding
all over the field of vision, they would still show
every variety of delicate tone and tint.

Weir Mitchell found that he could only see the visions with closed eyes and in a perfectly dark room.
I could see them in the dark with almost equal facility, though they were not of equal brilliancy, when
my eyes were wide open. I saw them best, however,
when my eyes were closed, in a room lighted only by
flickering firelight. This evidently accords with the
experience of the Indians, who keep a fire burning
brightly throughout their mescal rites.

The visions continued with undiminished brilliance for many hours, and as I felt somewhat faint
and muscularly weak, I went to bed, as I undressed
being greatly impressed by the red, scaly, bronzed,
and pigmented appearance of my limbs whenever I
was not directly gazing at them. I had not the faintest desire for sleep; there was a general hyperæsthesia of all the senses as well as muscular irritability,
and every slightest sound seemed magnified to startling dimensions. I may also have been kept awake

by a vague alarm at the novelty of my condition, and the possibility of further developments.

After watching the visions in the dark for some hours I became a little tired of them and turned on the gas. Then I found that I was able to study a new series of visual phenomena, to which previous observers had made no reference. The gas jet (an ordinary flickering burner) seemed to burn with great brilliance, sending out waves of light, which expanded and contracted in an enormously exaggerated manner. I was even more impressed by the shadows, which were in all directions heightened by flushes of red, green, and especially violet. The whole room, with its white-washed but not very white ceiling, thus became vivid and beautiful. The difference between the room as I saw it then and the appearance it usually presents to me was the difference one may often observe between the picture of a room and the actual room. The shadows I saw were the shadows which the artist puts in, but which are not visible in the actual scene under normal conditions of casual inspection. I was reminded of the paintings of Claude Monet, and as I gazed at the scene it occurred to me that mescal perhaps produces exactly the same conditions of visual hyperæsthesia, or rather exhaustion, as may be produced on the artist by the influence of prolonged visual attention. I wished to ascertain how the subdued and steady electric light would influence vision, and passed into the next room; but here the shadows were little marked, although walls and floor seemed tremulous and insubstantial, and the texture of everything was heightened and enriched.

About 3:30 a. m. I felt that the phenomena were distinctly diminishing—though the visions, now chiefly of human figures, fantastic and Chinese in character, still continued—and I was able to settle myself to sleep, which proved peaceful and dreamless. I awoke at the usual hour and experienced no sense of fatigue nor other unpleasant reminiscence of the experience I had undergone. Only my eyes seemed unusually sensitive to color, especially to blue and violet; I can, indeed, say that ever since this experience I have been more æsthetically sensitive than I was before to the more delicate phenomena of light and shade and color.

It occurred to me that it would be interesting to have the experiences of an artist under the influence of mescal, and I induced an artist friend to make a similar experiment. Unfortunately no effects whatever were produced at the first attempt, owing, as I have since discovered, to the fact that the buttons had only been simply infused and their virtues not extracted. To make sure of success the experiment was repeated with four buttons, which proved to be an excessive and unpleasant dose. There were paroxysmal attacks of pain at the heart and a sense of imminent death, which naturally alarmed the subject, while so great was the dread of light and dilation of the pupils that the eyelids had to be kept more or less closed, though it was evident that a certain amount of vision was still possible. The symptoms came on very suddenly, and when I arrived they were already at their height. As the experiences of this subject were in many respects very unlike mine, I will give them in his own words: "I noticed first that as I happened to turn my eyes away from a blue enamel kettle at which I had been unconsciously looking, and which was standing in the fender of the fireplace, with no fire in it, it seemed to me that I saw a spot of the same blue in the black coals of the grate, and that this spot appeared again, farther off, a little brighter in hue. But I was in doubt whether I had not imagined these blue spots. When, however, I lifted my eyes to the mantelpiece, on which were scattered all sorts of odds and ends, all doubt was over. I saw an intensely vivid blue light begin to play around every object. A square cigarette box, violet in color, shone like an amethyst. I turned my eyes away and beheld this time, on the back of a polished chair, a bar of color glowing like a ruby. Although I was expecting some such manifestation as one of the first systems of the intoxication, I was nevertheless somewhat alarmed when this phenomenon took place. Such a silent and sudden illumination of all things around, where a moment before I had seen nothing uncommon, seemed like a kind of madness beginning from outside me, and its strangeness affected me more than its beauty. A desire to escape from it led me to the door, and the act of moving had, I noticed, the effect of dispelling the colors. But a sudden difficulty in breathing and a sensation of numbness at the heart brought me back to the arm-chair from which I had risen. From this moment I had a series of attacks or paroxysms, which I can only describe by saying that I felt as though I were dying. It was impossible to move, and it seemed almost impossible to breathe. My speedy dissolution, I half imagined, was about to take place, and the power of making any resistance to the violent sensations that were arising within was going, I felt, with every second.

"The first paroxysms were the most violent. They would come on with tinglings in the lower limbs, and with the sensation of a nauseous and suffocating gas mounting up into my head. Two or three times this was accompanied by a color vision of the gas bursting into flame as it passed up my throat. But I seldom had visions during the paroxysms; these would appear in the intervals. They began with a spurting up of colors; once, of a flood of brightly illuminated green water covering the field of vision, and effervescing in parts, just as when fresh water with all the air bubbles is pumped into a swimming bath. At another time my eye seemed to be turning into a vast drop of dirty water in which millions of minute creatures resembling tadpoles were in motion. But the early visions consisted mostly of a furious succession of colored arabesques, arising and descending or sliding at every possible angle into the field of view. It would be as difficult to give a description of the whirl of water at the bottom of a waterfall as to describe the chaos of color and design which marked this period.

"Now also began another series of extraordinary sensations. They set in with bewildering suddenness and followed one another in rapid succession. These I now record as they occur to my mind at haphazard: (1) My right leg became suddenly heavy and solid; it seemed, indeed, as if the entire weight of my body had shifted into one part, about the thigh and knee, and that the rest of my body had lost all substantiality. (2) With the suddenness of a neuralgic pang, the back of my head seemed to open and emit streams of bright color; this was immediately followed by the feeling as of a draft blowing like a gale through the hair in the same region. (3) At one moment the color green acquired a taste in my mouth; it was sweetish and somewhat metallic; blue again would have a taste that seemed to recall phosphorous; these are the only colors that seemed to be connected with taste. (4) A feeling of delightful relief and preternatural lightness about my forehead, succeeded by a growing sensation of contraction. (5) Singing in one of my ears. (6) A sensation of burning heat in the palm of my left hand. (7) Heat about both eyes. The last continued throughout the whole period, except for a moment when I had a sensation of cold upon the eyelids, accompanied with a color vision of the wrinkled lid, of the skin disappearing from the brow, of dead flesh, and finally of a skull.

"Throughout these sensations and visions my mind remained not only perfectly clear, but enjoyed, I believe, an unusual lucidity. Certainly I was conscious of an odd contrast in hearing myself talk rationally with H[avelock] E[llis], who had entered the room a short time before, and experiencing at the same moment the wild and extraordinary pranks that were taking place in my body. My reason appeared to be the sole survivor of my being. At times I felt that this, too, would go, but the sound of my own voice would establish again the communication with the outer world of reality.

"Tremors were more or less constant in my lower limbs. Persistent, also, was the feeling of nausea. This, when attended by a feeling of suffocation and a pain at the heart, was relieved by taking brandy, coffee, or biscuit. For muscular exertion I felt neither the wish nor the power. My hands, however, retained their full strength.

"It was painful for me to keep my eyes open above a few seconds; the light of day seemed to fill the room with a blinding glare. Yet every object, in the brief glimpse I caught, appeared normal in color and shape. With my eyes closed, most of the visions, after the first chaotic display, represented parts of the whole of my body undergoing a variety of marvelous changes, of metamorphoses or illumination. They were more often than not comic and grotesque in character, though often beautiful in color. At one time I saw my right leg filling up with a delicate heliotrope; at another, the sleeve of my coat changed into a dark green material, in which was worked a pattern in red braid, and the whole bordered at the cuff with sable. Scarcely had my new sleeve taken shape than I found myself attired in a complete costume of the same fashion, mediæval in character, but I could not say to what precise period it belonged. I noted that a chance movement—of my

hand, for instance—would immediately call up a
color vision of the part exerted, and that this again
would pass, by a seemingly natural transition, into
another wholly dissimilar. Thus, pressing my fingers
accidentally against my temples, the fingertips became elongated, and then grew into the ribs of a
vaulting or of a dome-shaped roof. But most of the
visions were of a more personal nature. I happened
once to lift a spoonful of coffee to my lips, and as I
was in the act of raising my arm for that purpose a
vision flashed before my closed (or nearly closed)
eyes, in all the hues of the rainbow, of my arm separated from my body, and serving me with coffee
from out of dark and indefinite space. On another
occasion, as I was seeking to relieve slight nausea by
taking a piece of biscuit passed to me by H[avelock]
E[llis], it suddenly streamed out into blue flame.
For an instant I held the biscuit close to my leg. Immediately my trousers caught alight, and then the
whole of the right side of my body, from the foot to
the shoulder, was enveloped in waving blue flame. It
was a sight of wonderful beauty. But this was not all.
As I placed the biscuit in my mouth it burst out
again into the same colored fire and illuminated the
interior of my mouth, casting a blue reflection on the
roof. The light in the Blue Grotto at Capri, I am able
to affirm, is not nearly as blue as seemed for a short
space of time the interior of my mouth. There were
many visions of which I could not trace the origin.
There were spirals and arabesques and flowers, and
sometimes objects more trivial and prosaic in character. In one vision I saw a row of small white

flowers, one against the other like pearls of a necklace, begin to revolve in the form of a spiral. Every flower, I observed, had the texture of porcelain. It was at a moment when I had the sensation of my cheeks growing hot and feverish that I experienced the strangest of all the color visions. It began with feeling that the skin of my face was becoming quite thin and of no stouter consistency than tissue paper, and the feeling was suddenly enhanced by a vision of my face, paper-like and semitransparent and somewhat reddish in color. To my amazement I saw myself as though I were inside a Chinese lantern, looking out through my cheek into the room. Not long after this I became conscious of a change in the visions. Their tempo was more moderate, they were less frequent, and they were losing somewhat in distinctness. At the same time the feeling of nausea and of numbness was departing. A short period followed in which I had no visions at all, and experienced merely a sensation of heaviness and torpor. I found that I was able to open my eyes again and keep them fixed on any object in the room without observing the faintest blue halo or prism, or bar of glowing color, and that, moreover, no visions appeared on closing them. It was now twilight, but beyond the fact of not seeing light or color, either without or within, I had a distinct feeling that the action of the drug was at an end and that my body had become sober suddenly. I had no more visions, though I was not wholly free from abnormal sensations, and I retired to rest. I lay awake till the morning, and with the exception of the following night I scarcely slept for the next three days, but I can not say that I felt any signs of fatigue, unless, perhaps, on one of the days when my eyes, I noticed, became very susceptible to any indications of blue in an object. Of color visions, or of any approach to color visions, there was no further trace; but all sorts of odd and grotesque images passed in succession through my mind during part of the first night. They might have been the dreams of a Baudelaire or of an Aubrey Beardsley. I would see figures with prodigious limbs, or strangely dwarfed and curtailed, or impossible combinations such as five or six fish, the color of canaries, floating about in air in a gold wire cage. But these were purely mental images, like the visions seen in a dream by a distempered brain.

"Of the many sensations of which my body had been the theater during three hours, not the least strange was the feeling I experienced on coming back into a normal condition. The recovery did not proceed gradually, but the whole outer and inner world of reality came back, as it were, with a bound. And for a moment it seemed strange. It was the sensation—only much intensified—which everyone has known on coming out into the light of day from an afternoon performance at a theater, where one has sat in an artificial light of gas and lamps, the spectator of a fictitious world of action. As one pours out with the crowd into the street, the ordinary world, by force of contrast with the sensational scenes just witnessed, breaks in upon one with almost a sense of unreality. The house, the aspect of the street, even the light of day appear a little foreign for a few moments. During these moments everything strikes the mind as odd and unfamiliar, or at least with a greater degree of objectivity. Such was my feeling with regard to my old and habitual self. During the period of intoxication the connection between the normal condition of my body and my intelligence had broken—my body had become in a manner a stranger to my reason—so that now on reasserting itself it seemed, with reference to my reason, which had remained perfectly sane and alert, for a moment sufficiently unfamiliar for me to become conscious of its individual and peculiar character. It was as if I had unexpectedly attained an objective knowledge of my own personality. . . ."

I next made experiments on two poets, whose names are both well known. One is interested in mystical matters, an excellent subject for visions, and very familiar with various vision-producing drugs and processes. His heart, however, is not very strong. While he obtained the visions, he found the effects of mescal on his breathing somewhat unpleasant; he much prefers hasheesh, though recognizing that its effects are much more difficult to obtain. The other enjoys admirable health, and under the influence of mescal he experienced scarcely the slightest unpleasant reaction, but, on the contrary, a very marked state of well being and beatitude. He took somewhat less than three buttons, so that the results were rather less marked than in my case, but they were perfectly definite. He writes: "I have never seen a succession of absolutely pictorial visions with such precision and such unaccountability. It seemed as if a series of dissolving views were carried swiftly before me, all going from right to left, none corresponding with any seen reality. For instance, I saw the most delightful dragons, puffing out their breath straight in front of them like rigid lines of steam, and balancing white balls at the end of their breath! When I tried to fix my mind on real things, I could generally call them up, but always with some inexplicable change. Thus, I called up a particular monument in Westminster Abbey, but in front of it, to the left, knelt a figure in Florentine costume, like someone out of a picture of Botticelli; and I could not see the tomb without also seeing this figure. Late in the evening I went out on the Embankment and was absolutely fascinated by an advertisement of 'Bovril,' which went and came in letters of light on the other side of the river. I cannot tell you the intense pleasure this moving light gave me and how dazzling it seemed to me. Two girls and a man passed me, laughing loudly, and lolling about as they walked. I realized, intellectually, their coarseness, but visually I saw them, as they came under a tree, fall into the lines of a delicate picture; it might have been an Albert Moore. After coming in I played the piano with closed eyes and got waves and lines of pure color, almost always without form, though I saw one or two appearances which might have been shields or breastplates—pure gold, studded with small jewels in intricate patterns. All the time I had no unpleasant feelings whatever, except a very slight headache, which came and went. I slept soundly and without dreams."

The results of music in the case just quoted—together with the habit of the Indians to combine the drum with mescal rites, and my own observation that very slight jarring or stimulation of the scalp would affect the visions—suggested to me to test the influence of music on myself. I therefore once more put myself under the influence of mescal (taking a somewhat smaller dose than on the first occasion), and lay for some hours on a couch with my head more or less in contact with the piano, and with closed eyes directed toward a subdued light, while a friend played, making various tests, of his own devising, which were not explained to me until afterwards. I was to watch the visions in a purely passive manner, without seeking to direct them, nor was I to think about the music, which, so far as possible, was unknown to me. The music stimulated the visions and added greatly to my enjoyment of them. It seemed to harmonize with them, and, as it were, support and bear them up. A certain persistence and monotony of character in the music was required in order to affect the visions, which then seemed to fall into harmony with it, and any sudden change in the character of the music would blur the visions, as though clouds passed between them and me. The chief object of the tests was to ascertain how far a desire on the composer's part to suggest definite imagery would affect my visions. In about half the cases there was no resemblance, in the other half there was a distinct resemblance, which was sometimes very remarkable. This was especially the case with Schumann's music, for example, with his Waldscenen and

Kinderscenen; thus "The Prophet Bird" called up vividly a sense of atmosphere and of brilliant feathery bird-like forms passing to and fro, "A Flower Piece" provoked constant and persistent images of vegetation, while "Scheherazade" produced an effect of floating white raiment, covered by glittering spangles and jewels. In every case my description was, of course, given before I knew the name of the piece. I do not pretend that this single series of experiments proves much, but it would certainly be worth while to follow up this indication and to ascertain if any light is hereby thrown on the power of a composer to suggest definite imagery, or the power of a listener to perceive it.

It would be out of place here to discuss the obscure question as to the underlying mechanism by which mescal exerts its magic powers. It is clear from the foregoing descriptions that mescal intoxication may be described as chiefly a saturnalia of the specific senses, and, above all, an orgy of vision. It reveals an optical fairyland, where all the senses now and again join the play, but the mind itself remains a self-possessed spectator. Mescal intoxication thus differs from the other artificial paradises which drugs procure. Under the influence of alcohol, for instance, as in normal dreaming, the intellect is impaired, although there may be a consciousness of unusual brilliance; hasheesh, again, produces an uncontrollable tendency to movement and bathes its victim in a sea of emotion. The mescal drinker remains calm and collected amid the sensory turmoil around him; his judgment is as clear as in the normal state; he falls into no oriental condition of vague and voluptuous reverie. The reason why mescal is of all this class of drugs the most purely intellectual in its appeal is evidently because it affects mainly the most intellectual of the senses. On this ground it is not probable that its use will easily develop into a habit. Moreover, unlike most other intoxicants, it seems to have no special affinity for a disordered and unbalanced nervous system; on the contrary, it demands organic soundness and good health for the complete manifestation of its virtues.[2] Further, unlike the other chief substances to which it may be compared, mescal does not wholly carry us away from the actual world, or plunge us into oblivion; a large part of its charm lies in the halo of beauty which it casts around the simplest and commonest things. It is the most democratic of the plants which lead men to an artificial paradise. If it should ever chance that the consumption of mescal becomes a habit, the favorite poet of the mescal drinker will certainly be Wordsworth. Not only the general attitude of Wordsworth, but many of his most memorable poems and phrases cannot—one is almost tempted to say—be appreciated in their full significance by one who has never been under the influence of mescal. On all these

---

[2] It is ture, as many persons do not need to be reminded, that in neurasthenia and states of overfatigue, symptoms closely resembling the slight and earlier phenomena of mescal intoxication are not uncommon; but in such cases there is rarely any sense of well-being and enjoyment.

grounds it may be claimed that the artificial paradise of mescal, though less seductive, is safe and dignified beyond its peers.

At the same time it must be remembered that at present we are able to speak on a basis of but very small experience, so far as civilized men are concerned. The few observations recorded in America and my own experiments in England do not enable us to say anything regarding the habitual consumption of mescal in large amounts. That such consumption would be gravely injurious I cannot doubt. Its safeguard seems to lie in the fact that a certain degree of robust health is required to obtain any real enjoyment from its visionary gifts. It may at least be claimed that for a healthy person to be once or twice admitted to the rites of mescal is not only an unforgettable delight, but an educational influence of no mean value.

3. ‖ALDOUS HUXLEY

The Doors of Perception

Thus it came about that, one bright May morning, I swallowed four-tenths of a gram of mescalin dissolved in half a glass of water and sat down to wait for the results. . . .

The change which actually took place in [my] world was in no sense revolutionary. Half an hour after swallowing the drug I became aware of a slow dance of golden lights. A little later there were sumptuous red surfaces swelling and expanding from bright nodes of energy that vibrated with a continuously changing, patterned life. At another time the closing of my eyes revealed a complex of gray structures, within which pale bluish spheres kept emerging into intense solidity and, having emerged, would slide noiselessly upwards, out of sight. But at no time were there faces or forms of men or animals. I saw no landscapes, no enormous spaces, no magical growth and metamorphosis of buildings, nothing remotely like a drama or a parable. The other world to which mescalin admitted me was not the world of visions; it existed out there, in what I could see with my eyes open. The great change was in the realm of objective fact. What had happened to my subjective universe was relatively unimportant.

I took my pill at eleven. An hour and a half later, I was sitting in my study, looking intently at a small glass vase. The vase contained only three flowers—a full-blown Belle of Portugal rose, shell pink with a hint at every petal's base of a hotter, flamier hue; a large magenta and cream-colored carnation; and, pale purple at the end of its broken stalk, the bold heraldic blossom of an iris. Fortuitous and provisional, the little nosegay broke all the rules of traditional good taste. At breakfast that morning I had been struck by the lively dissonance of its colors. But that was no longer the point. I was not looking now at an unusual flower arrangement. I was seeing what Adam had seen on the morning of his creation—the miracle, moment by moment, of naked existence.

"Is it agreeable?" somebody asked. (During this part of the experiment, all conversations were recorded on a dictating machine, and it has been possible for me to refresh my memory of what was said.)

"Neither agreeable nor disagreeable," I answered. "It just *is*." . . .

I continued to look at the flowers, and in their living light I seemed to detect the qualitative equivalent of breathing—but of a breathing without returns to a starting point, with no recurrent ebbs but only a repeated flow from beauty to heightened beauty, from deeper to ever deeper meaning. Words like "grace" and "transfiguration" came to my mind, and this, of course, was what, among other things, they stood for. My eyes traveled from the rose to the carnation, and from that feathery incandescence to the smooth scrolls of sentient amethyst which were the iris. The Beatific Vision, *Sat Chit Ananda,* Being-Awareness-Bliss—for the first time I understood, not on the verbal level, not by inchoate hints or at a distance, but precisely and completely what those prodigious syllables referred to. . . .

"What about spatial relationships?" the investigator inquired, as I was looking at the books.

It was difficult to answer. True, the perspective looked rather odd, and the walls of the room no longer seemed to meet in right angles. But these were not the really important facts. The really important facts were that spatial relationships had ceased to matter very much and that my mind was perceiving the world in terms of other than spatial categories. At ordinary times the eye concerns itself with such problems as *Where?—How far?—How situated in relation to what?* In the mescalin experience the implied questions to which the eye responds are of another order. Place and distance cease to be of much interest. The mind does its perceiving in terms of intensity of existence, profundity of significance, relationships within a pattern. I saw the books, but was not at all concerned with their positions in space. What I noticed, what impressed itself upon my mind was the fact that all of them glowed with living light and that in some the glory was more manifest than in others. In this context position and the three dimensions were beside the point. Not, of course, that the category of space had been abolished. When I got up and walked about, I could do so quite normally, without misjudging the whereabouts of objects. Space was still there; but it had lost its predominance. The mind was primarily concerned, not with measures and locations, but with being and meaning.

And along with indifference to space there went an even more complete indifference to time.

"There seems to be plenty of it," was all I would answer, when the investigator asked me to say what I felt about time.

Plenty of it, but exactly how much was entirely irrelevant. I could, of course, have looked at my watch; but my watch, I knew, was in another universe. My actual experience had been, was still, of an indefinite duration or alternatively of a perpetual present made up of one continually changing apocalypse.

From the books the investigator directed my attention to the furniture. A small typing table stood in the center of the room; beyond it, from my point of view, was a wicker chair and beyond that a desk. The three pieces formed an intricate pattern of horizontals, uprights and diagonals—a pattern all the more interesting for not being interpreted in terms of spatial relationships. Table, chair and desk came together in a composition that was like something by Braque or Juan Gris, a still life recognizably related to the objective world, but rendered without depth, without any attempt at photographic realism. I was looking at my furniture, not as the utilitarian who has to sit on chairs, to write at desks and tables, and not as the cameraman or scientific recorder, but as the pure aesthete whose concern is only with forms and their relationships within the field of vision or the picture space. But as I looked, this purely aesthetic, Cubist's-eye view gave place to what I can only describe as the sacramental vision of reality. I was back where I had been when I was looking at the flowers—back in a world where everything shone with the Inner Light, and was infinite in its significance. The legs, for example, of that chair—how miraculous their tubularity, how supernatural their polished smoothness! I spent several minutes—or was it several centuries?—not merely gazing at those bamboo legs, but actually *being* them—or rather being myself in them; or, to be still more accurate (for "I" was not involved in the case, nor in a certain sense were "they") being my Not-self in the Not-self which was the chair. . . .

What happens to the majority of the few who have taken mescalin under supervision can be summarized as follows.

(1) The ability to remember and to "think straight" is little if at all reduced. (Listening to the recordings of my conversation under the influence of the drug, I cannot discover that I was then any stupider than I am at ordinary times.)

(2) Visual impressions are greatly intensified and the eye recovers some of the perceptual innocence of childhood, when the sensum was not immediately

and automatically subordinated to the concept. Interest in space is diminished and interest in time falls almost to zero.

(3) Though the intellect remains unimpaired and though perception is enormously improved, the will suffers a profound change for the worse. The mescalin taker sees no reason for doing anything in particular and finds most of the causes for which, at ordinary times, he was prepared to act and suffer, profoundly uninteresting. He can't be bothered with them, for the good reason that he has better things to think about.

(4) These better things may be experienced (as I experienced them) "out there," or "in here," or in both worlds, the inner and the outer, simultaneously or successively. That they *are* better seems to be self-evident to all mescalin takers who come to the drug with a sound liver and an untroubled mind.

"This is how one ought to see," I kept saying as I looked down at my trousers, or glanced at the jeweled books in the shelves, at the legs of my infinitely more than Van-Goghian chair. "This is how one ought to see, how things really are." And yet there were reservations. For if one always saw like this, one would never want to do anything else. Just looking, just being the divine Not-self of flower, of book, of chair, of flannel. That would be enough. But in that case what about other people? What about human relations? In the recording of that morning's conversations I find the question constantly repeated, "What about human relations?" How could one reconcile this timeless bliss of seeing as one

ought to see with the temporal duties of doing what
one ought to do and feeling as one ought to feel?
"One ought to be able," I said, "to see these trousers
as infinitely important and human beings as still
more infinitely important." One ought—but in practice it seemed to be impossible. This participation in
the manifest glory of things left no room, so to
speak, for the ordinary, the necessary concerns of
human existence, above all for concerns involving
persons. For persons are selves and, in one respect at
least, I was now a Not-self, simultaneously perceiving and being the Not-self of the things around me.
To this new-born Not-self, the behavior, the appearance, the very thought of the self it had momentarily
ceased to be, and of other selves, its one-time fel-
lows, seemed not indeed distasteful (for distasteful-
ness was not one of the categories in terms of which
I was thinking), but enormously irrelevant. Compelled by the investigator to analyze and report on
what I was doing (and how I longed to be left alone
with Eternity in a flower, Infinity in four chair legs
and the Absolute in the folds of a pair of flannel
trousers!), I realized that I was deliberately avoiding
the eyes of those who were with me in the room, deliberately refraining from being too much aware of
them. One was my wife, the other a man I respected
and greatly liked; but both belonged to the world
from which, for the moment, mescalin had delivered
me—the world of selves, of time, of moral judg-
ments and utilitarian considerations, the world (and
it was this aspect of human life which I wished,
above all else, to forget) of self-assertion, of cock-

sureness, of overvalued words and idolatrously worshiped notions. . . .

But meanwhile my question remained unanswered. How was this cleansed perception to be reconciled with a proper concern with human relations, with the necessary chores and duties, to say nothing of charity and practical compassion? The age-old debate between the actives and the contemplatives was being renewed—renewed, so far as I was concerned, with an unprecedented poignancy. For until this morning I had known contemplation only in its humbler, its more ordinary forms—as discursive thinking; as a rapt absorption in poetry or painting or music; as a patient waiting upon those inspirations, without which even the prosiest writer cannot hope to accomplish anything; as occasional glimpses, in Nature, of Wordsworth's "something far more deeply interfused"; as systematic silence leading, sometimes, to hints of an "obscure knowledge." But now I knew contemplation at its height. At its height, but not yet in its fullness. For in its fullness the way of Mary includes the way of Martha and raises it, so to speak, to its own higher power. Mescalin opens up the way of Mary, but shuts the door on that of Martha. It gives access to contemplation —but to a contemplation that is incompatible with action and even with the will to action, the very thought of action. In the intervals between his revelations the mescalin taker is apt to feel that, though in one way everything is supremely as it should be, in another there is something wrong. His problem is essentially the same as that which confronts the

quietist, the *arhat* and, on another level, the landscape painter and the painter of human still lives.
Mescalin can never solve that problem; it can only
pose it, apocalyptically, for those to whom it had
never before presented itself. The full and final
solution can be found only by those who are prepared to implement the right kind of *Welt-
anschauung* by means of the right kind of behavior
and the right kind of constant and unstrained alert-
ness.

4. R. C. ZAEHNER

From Somewhere to Nowhere

At my own request I was the subject of an experiment with mescalin on 3 December 1955. Dr. J. R. Smythies of the Psychological Laboratory, Cambridge, administered the drug and supervised my reactions. He was assisted by Mr. E. Osborn of the Society for Psychical Research. Also present were Dr. A. C. Allison, Student of Christ Church, and Mr. Alan Tyson, Fellow of All Souls, who is a student of psychology. The experiment took place in my own rooms in All Souls College, Oxford.

0.4 gram of mescalin was administered at 11:40 a.m. on 3 December. This was accompanied by ½ tablet of dramamine to prevent possible nausea. Before the drug took effort Dr. Smythies questioned me on previous hypnagogic experiences. I told him that, when dozing or before falling asleep, I frequently saw faces forming in front of me. These faces are usually dimly lit against a black ground: they form, stay for a few seconds, and then disappear. As one face disappears, another slowly takes its place and disappears in its turn, and so on. The faces are usually of one type (old or middle-aged women, less frequently men, practically never young men or women, never children). These faces are never familiar. Another phenomenon which occurs to me when dozing or before going to sleep is that I appear to be reading a book. I see the print clearly and distinguish the words, but the words rarely seem to have any particular significance. The books I appear to be reading are never books with which I am familiar, but frequently deal with whatever subject I have been reading during the day.

At 11:50 I was shown various objects and my reactions to them were noted. This was recorded on a tape-recorder, but the conversation is not sufficiently interesting to be reported in full. Three reproductions of Italian renaissance pictures, one of which I was later to see when under the influence of the drug, were shown to me. The one I was to look at later was a detail of the 'Adoration of the Magi' by Gentile da Fabriano (the original of which is in the Uffizi at Florence).

I explained that in this picture I was principally attracted by the richness of the colouring and the delicacy and sumptuousness of the draperies. I also looked at the best of my Persian rugs—a Feraghan of extraordinarily rich design with a basic colouring of deep, glowing russets—and said that I hoped to have a chance of examining it when the drug had 'taken', since it appeared that the one phenomenon common to most mescalin-takers was a pronounced heightening of the sense of colour. I also asked if I might listen to Berlioz's *Te Deum*, almost my favourite work in all music, 'which puts me into a manic state anyway'. The investigators then showed

me a Persian cigarette box of very ordinary work-
manship which I happen to possess, a wineglass
which, when held up to the light, shows a deep crimson, and, as a totally neutral object, an ink pot. I
further expressed a desire to see the dust-jacket of
the Nixa recording of Berlioz's *Symphonie Funèbre
et Triomphale*. This is divided into four unequal rec-
tangles, two brilliantly green, one brilliantly red, and
one black. In the red rectangle is reproduced a distorted version of Michelangelo's 'David' as far as the
navel; in the much smaller black rectangle is the
head of a Bellini Madonna. The 'David', as reproduced, I described as 'interesting in a sinister kind of
way'. I was also asked to look at a small cut-glass
decanter and a group of flowers which I had pur-
chased for the occasion.

At 12:55 no reaction had taken place except
light-headedness. I was asked to look intently at an
electric light bulb to test me for the after-image. As
I gazed at the bulb, it seemed to grow brighter and
to expand a little.[1] On shutting my eyes the after-
image behaved on more or less conventional lines—
starting as green in the centre of my visual field, it
ascended, appeared to explode, became red in the
middle and green outside. It changed colour so
often, exploded into a dim bluish pattern and re-
formed again so often that I could not describe these
metamorphoses quickly enough. The image that re-

---

[1] I have repeated this experiment subsequently and found
that the impression of increased brightness repeated itself,
and I even fancied the bulb grew a little larger.

mains most clearly in my memory is that of a slowly
mounting fiery ball which reminded me of an atomic
explosion. I thought it sinister and described it as
'horrid'. I disliked the experience and said that what
displeased me most was 'the fact that one's losing
control of oneself'. My conscious resistance to the
drug was, indeed, very strong, and this may account
for the fact that it took so long to operate.

At this point it should perhaps be stated that as
the day approached on which I was to take the drug,
I had become increasingly uneasy. I dreamt about it
three nights running and, quite irrationally, feared
either that it might be fatal, or that it might make me
permanently mad. These fears (which Mr. Raymond
Mortimer experienced when under the influence of
the drug) were not wholly serious and did not occur
at any point once the drug had begun to work. It is
true that it occurred to me at a later stage, when I
had a pronounced sensation of cold in my extremities and in my genitals, that I might quite possibly
die; but, in the curious state of mind I was then in
and which I shall attempt to describe, I considered
this of no possible interest to anyone, least of all to
myself. It seemed to me to be wholly God's affair
what happened to me, and I was very firmly convinced that He was merciful.

Shortly after the after-image experiment I asked
Mr. Tyson to take the investigators in turn down to
lunch. He took Mr. Osborn and left Dr. Smythies
with me. I was still suffering from nothing worse
than light-headedness and, accompanied by Dr.
Smythies, I took a stroll in the great quadrangle to

see whether the twin towers and the Radcliffe Camera were much as before: they were. I then took Dr. Smythies into the buttery for lunch and, according to those present, behaved in a perfectly normal manner. I did not myself eat nor did I feel any inclination to do so. We then proceeded to the coffee room where I had a little very weak coffee. I then suggested that, since the drug was taking so long to act, we might go for a stroll through Christ Church Meadow, finally debouching into Christ Church where I had successively been a scholar, senior scholar, and research lecturer. I was particularly anxious to do this as I hoped the drug would be beginning to work as we reached Christ Church and I wished to see what (if anything) happened to Tom Tower when seen under the influence of mescalin. I wished to do this because when I first saw it at the age of eighteen, it made a quite overwhelming impression on me. This impression I have never wholly lost.

We left All Souls at about 1:30 p.m., crossed the High without difficulty and walked down towards Magdalen. I was still feeling light-headed and felt that I was having some difficulty in controlling my legs. I pointed out objects of architectural interest and enlightened my guests (I still thought of them as guests rather than as medical supervisors) as to the state of the controversy about the Oxford inner relief roads. We turned into the Meadow at Rose Lane, and proceeded down the Broad Walk. In the High I had a curious sensation in my body which reminded me of what Mr. Custance describes as a 'tingling at the base of the spine' which, according to him, usu-

ally precedes a bout of mania. It was rather like
that. In the Broad Walk this sensation occurred, but
more strongly. It felt as if something warm were
surging up the body. The sensation occurred again
and again until the climax of the experiment was
reached, and in all cases after a period of quiescence.
I did not like it at all.

From the Broad Walk we turned right and
reached Merton Street. I now felt that the drug was
about to 'take': something was going to happen, but
not just yet, I thought. As I wanted 'things to happen' when I entered Tom Quad, I steered my guests
into Merton Chapel because I felt sure that the drug
needed a little time yet in which to act. The Chapel
was looking the same as usual: I looked at the very
beautiful east window, but was more conscious of
the damp and dank which do so much to mar that
noble edifice. I was also feeling rather giddy.

From Merton we proceeded to Christ Church
through Canterbury Gate and Peckwater Quad. On
emerging into Tom Quad, the moment I had been
eagerly anticipating, nothing happened at all. Tom
Tower stood there as he always has done, looking
precisely the same. I was rather disappointed that
my guests did not admire him more. We walked
along the east side of the quad and entered the Cathedral. I had no special interest in the Cathedral,
but since it is certainly the most beautiful mediæval
ecclesiastical interior in Oxford, I thought my guests
ought to be given the opportunity of seeing it, since
as a 'subject' I must, so far, have been a disappointment.

On entering the Cathedral things began to happen. I stood at the west end of the nave under the organ-loft and looked down into the choir. The choir terminates in a rose window above, below which is an arcade; below this again are two small Norman windows. The rose window and the lower windows contain very respectable nineteenth-century stained glass. As I looked, the rose window seemed to expand and contract rhythmically, its pattern continually changing meanwhile. The effect was interesting certainly, but seemed to me less beautiful than its normal state. After a short while I found this growing and shrinking annoying, and proceeded down the northern aisle. As I walked up it I noticed that the Burne-Jones window in front was also behaving in a curious manner. The window did not seem distinctly visible; it was as if there were thin veils of gossamer between me and it. On coming closer I was struck by the left-hand figure, a young man in profile with hand upraised. His head and hand moved slightly in the direction in which he was looking, but he could not get any farther because, it seemed to me, he was imprisoned in the glass. The patterns made by the actual pieces of glass were meanwhile leading a life independent of the life of the figures depicted on them. Like the pattern of the rose window they were perpetually on the move, forming and reforming, and not remaining still for a moment. It was rather like looking at figures through rippling water, but it was a kind of water that prevented the figures from doing what they wanted to do, hard though they tried to do it. Meanwhile the haloes of the four figures seemed to glow with an intenser lustre. This was, however, not so, for the other colours had all faded into various degrees of white and whitish grey. On returning to the Cathedral later the haloes seemed to be precisely as they were before, whereas all the rest had changed completely: under the influence of the drug they were drained of all positive colour.

Leaving the Burne-Jones I went to look at some mediæval glass in the Latin Chapel, but this refused to have anything to do with the drug, and remained obstinately itself. I then wished to look at the window at the west end of the north aisle since it contained vivid yellows and greens which I thought might seem more intense now that the drug had started to work. The window, however, looked, if anything, more drab than usual and I passed on back to the west end of the nave. There I took up my position again.

The rose window was still behaving in the same unusual way, expanding and contracting in a rhythmical manner. By now I found this irritating and transferred my attention to the centre of the choir's fan-vaulting. This I saw with absolute clarity; the pattern was simple and every detail was clearly etched. The stone seemed to be slightly more yellowish in the centre of my vision, though there was no change in the colourings of the surrounding pendants. I was astonished to find when I returned to the Cathedral that the pattern I had seen so clearly was not in fact the pattern as it actually is on the vault. What I had seen was very much simpler and less intricate. Though the pattern itself stayed absolutely still, everything else was in perpetual motion. At one time the whole choir would gently roll like a ship, sometimes in time with the organ (which was playing) and sometimes following a rhythm all its own. The roof of the choir, too, would expand and contract; and the pendants performed what seemed to be a ritual dance of their own, sometimes multiplying themselves, and sometimes coalescing. Meanwhile the rose window continued to expand and contract and interfered gravely with the figures being executed by the rolling choir as a whole and with the individual motions of the fan-vaulting. I was delighted with the choir's performance and distinctly annoyed by the rival performance put on by the rose window. It did not seem to me interesting or beautiful in itself and merely interfered with the grave dance of the stone-work. Whenever I transferred my glance to the top of the vault the same pattern appeared with absolute clarity and the dancing pendants fell rhythmically into place, pursuing their concerted life beneath it.

It was strange that though the choir was undergoing these delicate metamorphoses, the rest of the Cathedral remained motionless, including the arch that separated the choir from the transept which acted as a frame to the scene that was taking place beyond. One of the investigators then asked me to look at one of the nearer pillars in the nave. It remained absolutely motionless. I respected it for that.

At this point I wished to emerge into Tom Quad

to see whether Tom Tower was still behaving in a normal way. He was. We then proceeded to the grand staircase since I was very interested to know whether the fan-tracery there was behaving in the same way as the fan-vaulting in the Cathedral. I was surprised to see that it remained absolutely motionless, but seemed very much lower and less impressive than usual. This disappointed me as I thought my visitors would carry away a very poor opinion of Oxford architecture.

We then returned to the Cathedral and I looked at the Burne-Jones window at the west end of the south aisle. This behaved in precisely the same way as its companion at the other end of the Cathedral—the same forming and reforming of patterns, the same impression that the figures were trying to fight themselves free of the glass, the same reduction of all colours to shades of white and whitish grey, the same persistent glowing of the reds.

I would have liked to have stayed in this magical Cathedral a little longer, but the investigators considered that it was time to return to All Souls. Both Tom Quad and Peckwater looked much as usual, though, when I returned to them the next day, they looked grander and more impressive than they had under the influence of the drug. By this time I had no difficulty at all in walking but had a curious sensation that my body was under perfect control, which seemed odd, for I was certainly, I thought, in no position to control it. The body seemed momentarily to be leading an autonomous life of its own—and very well it managed it—whereas 'I' was becoming increasingly confused and unsure of myself. On reaching the High, I felt very grateful for the presence of my companions; for, though there was not overmuch traffic, I was not absolutely certain that what I saw was actually there.

* * *

On returning to my rooms I sat down, feeling rather tired. The time was now 2:45, and the investigators tried to elicit a more or less clear account of my experiences in the Cathedral.

'In the Cathedral,' I replied, 'I started looking at the rose window which at first seemed to be fairly clear and then it faded. . . . I'm sorry, things are coming a bit odd. . . . I don't seem to be able to remember, I can't express myself any more. . . . I'm not feeling very . . . er . . . sensible at the moment.'

I was then asked about things around me and how they were behaving. I was feeling rather exhausted and had some difficulty in replying.

'They're going up and down rather,' I said, '. . . very misty . . . the bookcase pattern forms and reforms. I wish it'd stay where it was. Dr. Allison is recognizable, I'm glad to say . . . (sigh). I'm sorry to look at you like this . . . (another sigh). Things are just *queer*. They don't stay in the same place very long, but they don't change very much.' In actual fact, though Dr. Allison's face was much the same, his right ear had expanded quite considerably, but I somehow felt it would be impolite to draw attention to this.

I was then asked to look at the Gentile da Fabriano 'Adoration of the Magi'. At first it looked 'precisely as it was before', and for some time remained so. 'Nothing seems to happen,' I remarked in a bored voice; then 'the second Magi (*sic*) moved his hand quite a lot then. He's bringing up the . . . no. (Testily) Come on, come on, come on (encouraging the Magus). He's trying to get up . . . doesn't make it. Trying to take his crown off . . . (deep breathing). . . . On the whole it stays very like the picture it really is. He's out of focus, the middle one; he has moved. . . . He was much more up this way a little while ago. . . . He's bending down a bit.'

Investigator. 'Any more solid, would you say?'

R. C. Z. 'More solid? I should say a little . . . yes . . . yes. It's not the same picture and yet it isn't, you know (*sic*) . . . (sighs). . . . Colour, I suppose, a little intenser. Not much.' The reason why the picture wasn't the same was, I think, that though nothing was now moving, parts of it were expanding and others contracting almost imperceptibly.

I was looking at the picture by daylight, and the investigators now shone a lamp on it. At this the picture appeared to come to life. It was the second Magus again who started it. He again moved his outstretched hand slightly forward and seemed to be trying hard to take his crown off. I half hoped that he would take it off, but since he didn't, I realized that *of course* he couldn't because he couldn't get out of the picture any more than the figures in the Cathedral could get out of their glass. But whereas I felt sympathetic to the figures in the Cathedral, the poor Magus' predicament seemed to me wildly amusing. In any case I now broke into uncontrollable laughter which was to last, on and off, for over an hour. The occasion for this excessive hilarity was, I suppose, the Magus; but this did not seem wholly clear to me at the time.

'What do you find so funny, Professor Zaehner?' an investigator asked:

R. C. Z. (ecstatically). 'Nothing.' This was true: everything had suddenly become so totally funny that to single out one thing rather than another would not at all have conveyed this experience of total funniness. I could only continue to laugh till I cried. The situation was not made one bit better by the behaviour of the Magi. The eldest, who is represented as kneeling and about to kiss the Infant Jesus' feet, seemed to advance while the Child attempted to push him back. And now it became clear that the Magus was not going to kiss the Child's feet: he was trying to bite them and the Child would not let him. Perhaps because, as I explained to the investigators before the experiment began, I had always admired this picture for the beauty and richness of its colouring, not for its religious content, I was not shocked by the thought of the Magus biting the feet of the Infant Jesus. I simply did not connect this grotesque scene with the actual subject of the picture. Even in my manic state I made a clear distinction between the world of 'funniness' and objects or pictures which seemed to me genuinely sacred. This will appear in the sequel.

When this initial laughing fit had subsided I looked round and complained:

R. C. Z. 'You all look so serious.'

Investigator. 'We can't enjoy it to the same extent you can.'

R. C. Z. (convulsed). 'No, I suppose you can't.' (Further gusts of uncontrollable laughter.)

Attempts were made to interest me in other pictures, but without success. 'I don't mind what I do,' I said, but really meant that I just wanted to laugh on in peace, 'laughing at nothing' as I described it. Efforts to interest me in books were equally vain until it became clear that the investigators wished to test whether I was still able to read correctly. This seemed worth trying. Things were still moving about in an inconsequential way though the majority of them stood still. It would be interesting to see what words were doing on the printed page. Finally I was induced to start reading the opening passage of Proust's *Du Côté de chez Swann*. The words and lines were, indeed, up to the oddest tricks; they seemed to be in a state of perpetual flux and it required a great effort to find the right line and to stick to it once found. I read, or rather chanted, the first paragraph more or less correctly. It came out like this:

' "Longtemps je me suis couché de bonne heure. Parfois, à peine ma bougie éteinte, mes yeux se fermaient si vite que je n'avais pas le temps de me dire: Je m'endors."—I wish to say that I am not doing anything of the kind.—"Et une demi-heure après, la pensée qu'il était temps de chercher le sommeil m'éveillait."—That can't be right.—"Je voulais poser le volume . . ." come on, volume (pronounced as

French), where do you want to be posé-ed?' The lines and words were now inextricably mixed up, which accounts for the last remark. ' ". . . que je croyais avoir encore dans les mains et souffler la lumière." This is one of the stupid things I read in my dreams.' (More laughter.)

Investigator. 'You do that in your dreams, do you?'

R. C. Z. (astonished at his naïveté). Don't be silly. It's the sort of thing I *read* in my dreams. I wish Proust was half as funny as that. . . . I'd give. . . . Take him away.' (Much laughter throughout.)

Investigator. 'Would you like another book?'

R. C. Z. 'No, they're all the same.'

Investigator. 'All rather stupid?'

R. C. Z. 'It doesn't seem to make much difference, the words change round anyhow.'

I then asked Dr. Allison what the book was which made his wife laugh so much when she was my pupil (she had been). He could not tell me, so I dismissed the matter with a favourable comment on his wife: 'She was a good girl.' Silence for a few moments, then:

R. C. Z. 'I wish everyone wasn't being so unfriendly.'

Investigator. 'Do we seem unfriendly?'

R. C. Z. (loudly and emphatically). 'Frightfully.' (Prolonged and uproarious laughter.)

More books were pressed on me and immediately rejected. 'Take it away, it's psycho-analysis.' Finally I was offered the first volume of *The Golden Bough*. Opening at p. 17 I saw the words 'Diana & Virbius' which I read as 'Diana and Virbio', a conjunction that struck me as being quite excruciatingly funny.

I read the paragraph starting 'Among the ancient Celts of Gaul . . .' more or less correctly, but with great difficulty because the words were behaving in an even more unruly manner than they had in Proust. Finally I could make nothing of it, but at last the word 'ancestors' seemed to stand still.

R. C. Z. 'The ancestors are settling down now. They're, they're, they're staying in the same place for one moment. Nice of them. Jolly nice of them. (Uncontrollable laughter.) This is the silliest test I have ever had to go through. You all take it so seriously. (Laughter.) Really you shouldn't be so serious. It's Diana, you see. (More uncontrollable laughter.) Here, wait a minute. (This addressed to the book.) "She did not reign alone in her grove at Nemi. Two lesser divinities shared her forest sanctuary. One was Egeria, the nymph of the clear water which, bubbling from the basaltic rocks, used to fall in graceful cascades into the mills of the modern village of Nemi mentioned by Ovid." Oh, that's clever of him. (Squeaks of delight.) This is quite an interesting book. What is it? Oh, *The Golden Bough.* Very funny. (More uncontrollable laughter.) One of the great comic classics.'

However, Diana appeared to have served her purpose: 'We've *had* her, let's go on to something different.' Turning the pages I was much distressed by the fact that Sir James Frazer's paragraphs were so long. 'Why doesn't he split his paragraphs?' I testily enquired. 'They're all over the place. . . . It's all wrong. I was brought up as an undergraduate not to do such a thing. Wicked.' I then started to read on p. 272:

'"The reader will observe"—I hope he jolly well will too (more uncontrollable laughter)—"how exactly the Japs . . . Javanese . . . try to make rain from the antithesis of Indian observations."' I then read a sentence more or less correctly, but was once again defeated by the mobility of the print. When the book seemed to settle down for a bit, I was slightly annoyed: 'They're moving again now, it's much funnier.' The following sentence, 'It is the old fallacy that the effect resembles its cause', brought on a wild paroxysm of mirth. This struck me as being really exceptionally funny. The idea that there actually still were people who believed in causes and effects, seemed to me grotesque: how could people be so silly? 'Oh, this is stupid,' I exclaimed. 'Oh, the man's playing the fool.'

The quotations from Sir James Frazer, it will have been observed, went a little wrong. This was because I was no longer master of the mobile print, I could no longer distinguish the right line, and the resultant nonsense seemed to me far more satisfying than what was actually written although that too, heaven knows, was funny enough.

I now asked Tyson for a glass of water since the quite immoderate amount of laughing I had been doing, had made me very thirsty. On Tyson's return:

R. C. Z. 'I was about to tell you my great thoughts about it. I'll think twice about that because . . .'

Tyson. 'What were they?'

R. C. Z. 'No, no, it's all right. I'll tell you when they come again.' In actual fact I did not disclose the 'great thought' because even then it seemed trite and amounted only to 'Everything is much funnier than it seems'.

Throughout this manic period I had been suffering from a feeling of cold in my extremities and also in my genitals. The cold feeling seemed to be creeping up my legs. It was slightly unpleasant, but in no way alarming.

Investigator. 'This is very like the record of the laughing policeman, do you know it?'

R. C. Z. 'Is it funny?'

Investigator. 'Very funny indeed.'

R. C. Z. 'Bet it isn't.' (Giggles, long pause.) 'Where's Charles?'[1]

Tyson. 'I expect he's in his rooms.'

R. C. Z. 'Let him stay there. You should ask him to be on time. Two seconds ago I'd have been pleased to see Charles. If he hasn't got the civility to turn up when he is wanted' (remainder incomprehensible owing to hysterical laughter).

Investigator. 'How does the water taste?'

R. C. Z. 'Rather like water, I'm afraid. I'm just rather dehydrated. . . . Is that the right word? . . . Hydration taking place . . . oh dear . . .' (giggles).

Investigator. 'How are the feet?'

R. C. Z. 'Oh, as cold as ever.' (Sighs.)

Investigator. 'Do you have any other sensations?'

R. C. Z. 'No . . . only laughter, if you call that a

---

[1] Charles Monteith, Fellow of All Souls.

sensation. (Laughter.) Cold feet, certainly. Jolly cold feet. . . . Oh dear! They're crooked too.'

Investigator. 'They're crooked?'

R. C. Z. 'Not more than usual, I don't think.'

Investigator. 'You're holding them crooked.'

R. C. Z. 'It doesn't seem to make much difference which way you hold them if they're crooked when you start.' (Uncontrollable laughter.)

At this stage the investigator tried to interest me in a Persian carpet which lies in front of the fireplace. The design is a medallion on a rich crimson ground.

R. C. Z. 'It's just the old rose window all over again, isn't it?'

Investigator. 'It's not quite the same as the rose window: it's nearer for one thing.'

R. C. Z. (emphatically). 'It's *just* the same. Just a dull old thing sitting in the middle of a spider's web.'

I was again asked to look at it.

R. C. Z. 'I don't want to look at the thing.'

Asked to look at the books, I said:

'Don't want to look at the books: why should I want to look at the books?'

Investigator. 'Describe what's going on there.'

R. C. Z. 'Why should anything go on there? Just a lot of books.'

On being asked to note any peculiarity of colour or shape I replied wearily:

'I don't think anything like that's going to happen. I'm quite prepared for these things to happen, but I don't think they do much.'

Investigator. 'When you say it's just like the rose

window, you mean it's behaving like it?'

R. C. Z. 'No, it just shows it's shoddy stuff.'

Investigator. 'Why, this isn't shoddy stuff, is it?'

R. C. Z. 'I *know*, I paid for it.' (Uncontrollable laughter.) 'I know that wasn't funny, but it seemed so to me.'

Tyson then showed me E. M. Forster's *Hill of Devi*. I had met Mr. Forster the previous year and liked him very much, and Tyson reminded me of the fact. After attempts at polite and more or less sane conversation on the subject of Mr. Forster's health, I concluded in an aggressive tone: 'He's a *very nice man*.' Turning to the frontispiece, a portrait of the Indian Prince under whom Mr. Forster served, I observed sagely, 'He knew about chaps, this one. . . . Nice silly man.'

The time was now 3:30.

I was now shown a reproduction of Michelangelo's 'Holy Family'.

R. C. Z. 'Now I suppose I'm meant to make intelligent comments on this.'

Investigator. 'Is there any movement there?'

R. C. Z. 'No. . . . I can't think why you expect things to move.' (Uncontrollable laughter.) 'Except that I do.'

Investigator. 'Do you?'

R. C. Z. 'Of course I don't, I mean unless they happen to be moving, you wouldn't expect them to, would you?'

I heard Allison say something like, 'There's quite a lot of method in this madness.'

R. C. Z. 'Don't whisper behind the scenes, it's

rude. (Sighs) . . . Ah! . . . (sighs deeply) . . .
I've got to go on looking at this, have I? I *knew*
they'd try and make me look at these ruddy things.
Why *should* I look at these things? . . . Silly. Oh,
I'm sorry . . . (laughter). . . . Native manners
overcome drug . . .' (more laughter).

More pictures were shown me but with little effect
until I asked to look at reproductions of Raphael's
'Deposition.' I fetched the book myself since no one
else could find it. I had no difficulty in moving about.
Running through the details I had no desire to laugh.

R. C. Z. 'All much too serious. . . . This is because it's a really serious picture.' This was the first
time I had stopped laughing since looking at the
Gentile da Fabriano. The reason was that Raphael is
to me an essentially religious and 'numinous' painter.
I was still in a world of nonsensical fantasy, and I
realized that Raphael could not fit in there—not for
me at any rate. The original of the picture is in the
Borghese Gallery in Rome and I had not long ago
looked at the picture with the present Warden of All
Souls. The investigators asked me to describe where
the original was. I could not remember the name of
the Borghese Gallery nor could I describe where it
was.

R. C. Z. 'Can't remember where it was . . .
(sighs). . . . How can I describe it? How can you
describe anything when you can't remember what
they're called? . . . Ring up the Warden, he knows.
. . . Precious little response to that one . . .
(laughter) . . . (peremptorily): Ring him up. . . .
I suppose I'll have to ring him up myself. . . .

What? (loud and annoyed) . . . I'll go and see the
Warden when he wants to see me, and I don't think
that'll be till tomorrow afternoon. (Uncontrollable
laughter.) No. Oh, I've got to look at this, haven't I?
I know you keep trying to make things happen, but
they don't *want* to happen. . . . That's where you're
all wrong. . . .' This remark, mad though it was,
reflected one of my basic convictions, namely, that it
is wrong to try to make others behave in a way that
is not natural to them. In my manic state, 'things'
had come to life and should therefore be treated with
the respect due to living organisms. I was not quite
mad enough not to realize that they were not really
alive: even so, I really did think it wrong to interfere
with them if they (like myself) happened to want to
rest.

At this point I suddenly wanted to have a look at
the dust-jacket of the *Symphonie Funèbre et Triomphale*:

R. C. Z. 'Oh, let's have a look at that silly old
creature we talked about before we took the drug.
(Laughter). . . . Oh, the *Symphonie Funèbre et
Triomphale,* but *not* the *Symphonie Funèbre et
Triomphale* but the dust-jacket of the *Symphonie
Funèbre et Triomphale* . . . (triumphantly) and if
that's not clear, I don't know what is. (More laughter). . . . See if he's going to dance around. (Looking at the dust-jacket.) Just shows him up, you see,
stupid old thing. Just nothing there at all, you see.
No good, can't get away with it, can't get away with
it. Just tripe, like everything else.'

Investigator. 'End of art.'

I was now handed the Phaidon Press edition of Berenson's *Italian Painters of the Renaissance*. I opened it at p. 114 where there is a colour reproduction of a praying figure from Piero della Francesca's 'Nativity' in the National Gallery.

R. C. Z. 'This bloke I really do think has got something, or at least I used to.'

Investigator. 'Do you enjoy looking at that?'

R. C. Z. 'I wish you'd leave me alone. . . . You keep interrupting.'

Still, as far as I remember, looking at the same picture, I said:

R. C. Z. 'Let's have a look at her . . . (sighs). . . . If you want to know what I feel about that, it's a holy thing not to be looked at when you're drugged.'

A book of reproductions of Picasso drawings was now produced and opened at an abstract black and white design.[1] The design at once sprang to life and the pattern moved about and changed continually:

Investigator. 'What do you think this particular thing shows?'

R. C. Z. (defiantly). 'Shows *what?*'

Investigator. 'Well . . . can you recognize anything in it?'

R. C. Z. 'Well, if it would stay still for a minute I might . . . extraordinary. . . . No, why should I

---

[1] *L'Œuvre gravé de Picasso,* La Guilde du Livre, Lausanne, 1955, p. 137.

recognize anything? It was all right when it was moving, but now it's stopped still, it's just silly. (Turns pages and comes to rest on pp. 106-7). . . . Ah, those chaps are coming up. . . . Slightly indecent. No . . . no. . . . (Turns more pages and comes to rest at p. 47). . . . Really people shouldn't twist themselves up so. (Laughs, then sighs. Turns to p. 78.) There's the good old collective unconscious looking out.' (General laughter.)

Investigator. 'What do you think of this?' (I think we had now moved to p. 104.)

R. C. Z. 'Oh, that girl, she's got all the right things. Even she's bloody dull. That's the trouble with Jung, he doesn't realize how dull his collective unconscious is . . . (laughs). . . . Well, I'm sorry you can't interest me in anything. (To the picture) Oh don't make mouths at me, don't be silly. . . . Yes. . . . Oh, this is the sort of thing that goes on when I fall asleep. Just this sort of racket exactly. Yes, they fit into a pattern. Do be one face and not another. I know you're doing your best, I know you're doing your best. . . . Come on; well, you want to be a Red Indian, do you? All right, all right, I'm not stopping you. All right. Yes, you're settling down. Yes, yes. Very nice Red Indian you are too. That's right. Now you can go away . . . (picture fades slightly). . . . Better . . . un. . . . Settling down, settling down. . . . (testily) Come on. (Same image emerges) We've had you before. It's no good, no good. No. She's back again. I'm afraid it's because there's a picture at the bottom of it and not just nothing at all. (Looking at picture on opposite page) Ah, this bloke's interesting, he doesn't seem to have got a nose. Doesn't seem to fit together much. . . . (bored) Oh, it's a Picasso, that's why. (General laughter.) . . . If you give me a picture of absolutely nothing at all, I might be able to make something of it.' (Uncontrollable laughter.)

The investigators now tried me on the Rorschach test.

R. C. Z. 'Oh, why were you so interested in that bottle of ink before lunch, anyhow?'

Investigator. 'Just a neutral object.'

R. C. Z. (decidedly). '*Very* neutral, I should think.'

The drug was now beginning to wear off, I think. Looking back on it, my reasoning (if such it can be called) seems to have been rather like this. Ever since the drug had started to work things depicted seemed to be trying to escape from the material in which they were depicted. They were trying to come to life, but never quite succeeded. However much the material might move, the figure imprisoned in it could never get free. The more definite the figure was, the less able was it to escape; yet if it was not at all definite, no recognizable figure emerged. The only solution appeared to be a confrontation with 'a picture of absolutely nothing at all'. Yet when confronted with the inky mess known as a Rorschach, I became totally uninterested. I was not able or willing to impose an image on to it, since basically I wanted the actual figures represented to come to life and behave as they wanted to behave. I did not want to impose figures of my own, hence I found myself incapable of visualizing anything at all.

As the Rorschach was being prepared, Mr. Stuart Hampshire came in.

R. C. Z. (hearing someone come in). 'Who's that? Charles? Oh, Stuart, hallo, old boy.' Here follows a cascade of really manic laughter. The reason for this was, I think, that Hampshire had come in and was behaving as he ordinarily does. This was immensely reassuring since I was perfectly well aware that the rest of them were not behaving naturally at all. They were investigating my reactions and trying (oh, so obviously) to humour a lunatic. Hence the uncontrolled joy with which I greeted Hampshire.

R. C. Z. 'Stuart, don't let them take you in.' This needs some explanation. There had been some question of Hampshire's taking the drug since the reactions of philosophers were likely to be of interest. I wished to tell Hampshire that he really need not waste his time since all the drug did was to reduce everything to the level of pure farce:

R. C. Z. 'Everything is very funny indeed.' (More uncontrollable laughter.)

S. N. H. 'How long has this been lasting?'

R. C. Z. 'Oh, quite a time. Ever since the Cathedral stopped going round . . . (peremptorily to Tyson who had already supplied, on request, endless glasses of water) Alan, water. . . . If you laugh as much as that and sweat as much as I do, you need an awful lot of water . . . (uncontrollable laughter). Physiological fact.'

Tyson now returned with a glass of water. The room seemed to be getting awfully full of people and it brought the cabin scene of the Marx Brothers' film 'A Night at the Opera' vividly to my mind:

R. C. Z. 'Ah, this is getting like a Marx Brothers' film . . . (general laughter). . . . Endless glasses of water . . .' (uncontrollable laughter).

The Rorschach was now handed to me:

Investigator. 'That's a Rorschach.'

R. C. Z. 'You've been working all out for me, have you? Now what's supposed to happen to this?'

Investigator. 'This is a . . . ink blot.'

R. C. Z. 'Ink blot . . . there seem to me a great many ink blots. Would you mind getting me some blotting paper?'

Investigator. 'It's just a bit damp in the middle.'

R. C. Z. 'It looks jolly wet to me.'

Investigator. 'A very, very small damp bit in the middle.'

R. C. Z. 'It's wet, not just damp.'

Investigator. 'No, just damp.'

R. C. Z. 'It looks *very* wet to me. What do you expect to happen to the silly thing for heaven's sake? . . . Well, if you'ld only let me get some control of myself instead of drugging an honest chap . . . (laughter). . . . There, here am I. . . . This is supposed to be a serious test . . . (more laughter). . . . No . . . oh, dear. Oh, gosh, my feet are so cold . . . oh dear . . . I wish there wasn't this tomb-like silence around one every time one opens one's mouth. . . .' (Laughter.)

S. N. H. 'There's a feeling you ought to say some great things from time to time.'

This was the sort of remark that made sense to

me. At least Hampshire was not trying to make me do all kinds of things I didn't want to do: he wasn't continually thrusting pictures into my hands and talking about those idiotic Rorschachs. This explains the following remark:

R. C. Z. 'Stuart's about the only person who talks a word of sense in this room.'

Here I once again burst into uncontrollable laughter, walked up and down the room (quite steadily) laughing and laughing and laughing. Observing the Feraghan rug hanging on the wall, I noticed delightedly that it was precisely the same as ever. That would teach these silly investigators, I thought, not to try and play tricks with my property. The investigators had by now become identified with the drug and I resented both the drug and the investigators. I fear I was very trying to them.

Since I was now incapable of doing anything but laugh, Hampshire took his leave with an encouraging smile (it was his own smile, and that pleased me quite extraordinarily and somehow proved that here was one man at least who didn't try to make people and things do what they didn't want to do).

N.B. The tape-recording comes to an end at this point which was, I suppose, the climax of my manic phase.

Efforts were now made to induce me to listen to music. This produced the usual negative reaction. I sat down again, apathetically refusing to be interested in anything. I was asked to close my eyes and to try to visualize something I liked. I could think of nothing whatever I liked. The investigators then suggested a glass of water, large quantities of which I had been drinking. Try as I might I could visualize absolutely nothing. The investigators now no longer seemed to want to interest me in things. Their tactics were wise, for I finally suggested myself that Berlioz's *Te Deum* be played on the gramophone. I was still very conscious of the cold in my feet which had now spread to the hands, genitals, and lower abdomen, and which seemed to be creeping up my legs. This I found vaguely disquieting, thought it might be dangerous, but didn't mind if it was.

I wasn't sure about the *Te Deum*. Perhaps it would be boring like everything else. Yet the moment the music went on, I was completely absorbed. It is a magnificently noisy work, and the moment it started, I knew I just wanted to lie limply in my chair and let the music in, choirs, brass, tympani, and all. The 'phenomena' had not stopped. Things, and particularly the lines on the fireplace, refused to stand still, my feet and hands were still as cold as ever, and at one stage my left hand looked half its normal size. These were now no more than irritating distractions. I closed my eyes, but patterns—though very inoffensive and indeterminate ones—continued to form. On opening them again the lines on the fireplace were up to their old tricks. As the *Te Deum* came near to its end, however, things settled down and I found I felt very exhausted but wide awake. Otherwise I felt absolutely all right and declined Dr. Smythies's kind offer of a sleeping pill.

Berlioz's *Te Deum* has, for me, religious as well as musical significance; and the fact that I asked for it to be played showed that at that stage I felt the manic phase had passed sufficiently for me to think about religious things. In the manic stage Raphael had stopped the laughter and the praying figure of Piero della Francesca had elicited the sane remark 'It's a holy thing not to be looked at when you're drugged'. Berlioz seemed to bridge the two worlds. Before the experiment I had said that his *Te Deum* 'puts me into a manic state anyway'. A friend of mine who came in just before the work began, agreed that that was the effect it had on him. To me it was quite different; it brought me back to the real world, slowly and surely, without violent transition. My only regret was that I should still be distracted from the music, the full strength and beauty of which I felt I was missing.

During the performance of the first side of the *Te Deum* I became increasingly conscious of the cold in my feet and hands. I thought that if this cold should reach my heart, I would probably die. This thought did not worry me at all, and I felt strongly that this was God's concern, not mine, and that He would certainly be merciful.

* * * * *

I would not presume to draw any conclusions from so trivial an experience. It was interesting and it certainly seemed hilariously funny. All along, however, I felt that the experience was in a sense 'anti-religious', I mean, not conformable with religious experience or in the same category. In Huxley's terminology 'self-transcendence' of a sort did take place, but transcendence into a world of farcical meaninglessness. All things were one in the sense that they were all, at the height of my manic state, equally funny: the quality of 'funniness' and incongruity had swallowed up all others. I was never frightened, and as, under the influence of Berlioz, I slowly returned to sanity, my normal religious consciousness, which was never completely swamped, returned in full vigour. There was no longer any reason why I should be afraid.

I would not wish to take the drug again, but purely on moral grounds. I should be most interested to know whether the drug taken elsewhere and in a different and less friendly environment would produce different effects; but the more the experience fades into the past, the clearer does it seem to me that, in principle, artificial interference with consciousness is, except for valid medical reasons, wrong.

5. ‖ CHRISTOPHER ISHERWOOD

A Visit to Anselm Oakes

Introduction by Christopher Isherwood: I think *A Visit to Anselm Oakes* explains itself sufficiently, and can be read without reference to anything else, as an adventure in hashish-taking. However, it was once part of *Down There on a Visit.*

In *Paul,* the final episode of that novel, the narrator, who is called Christopher Isherwood, goes to visit Paul in Paris and finds him taking opium. Christopher tries to be very broadminded about this. He even offers to smoke a pipe himself, in order to understand the occult experiences which Paul hints that he is having. Paul is scornfully amused. 'You're exactly like a tourist,' he tells Christopher, 'who thinks he can take in the whole of Rome in one day. You know, you really *are* a tourist, to your bones. I bet you're always sending postcards with "down here on a visit" on them. That's the story of your life. . . .'

In the version which contains the encounter with Anselm Oakes, Paul finally relents and says that, after all, he may just possibly be able to help Chris 'see something'. He proposes taking Chris to meet Anselm, who writes books on witchcraft, and makes a living out of peddling psychic mumbo-jumbo to suckers and giving hashish parties at which the guests must pay an 'initiation fee'.

Paul tells Chris that he has realized he will never understand goodness until he can understand evil; so he has been hunting around for someone who really *is* evil, so far without complete success. Several people recommended Anselm to him; but, when Paul met Anselm, he was disappointed. All he has got from Anselm, he says, are 'a few hints'.

Christopher, as will be seen, is equally disappointed in Anselm at first. Then, under the influence of the hashish, he does get a glimpse of Evil, not only in Anselm but also in his fellow-guests. But wherein does this Evil actually reside? In Anselm, or in Christopher himself, or in Paul, who, with characteristic sadism, has told Mokhtar to prepare the drug in such a way as to plunge Chris into the horrors of 'Down There'?

Not long before the novel was published, in 1962, I suddenly decided to take the visit to Anselm out of it. This section is almost exclusively about Chris and his experiences; it does not really belong to the story of Paul.

Gigi is Paul's dog. Augustus cannot be described so succinctly. If you want to know who he is, you must read the novel.

Anselm Oakes lived way out in the suburbs, somewhere near Meudon. It took an immensely long taxi ride to get us there; and first we had to drop Gigi off at the Rue de Bac. 'I don't trust Anselm,' Paul told me, half seriously: 'I know he's got his eye on her.

He wants to sacrifice her to a devil he likes, called Eazaz.'

At last we arrived at a block of modernistic flats, perhaps not more than fifteen years old, but already dilapidated. The elevator came down very slowly, making sounds as if its shaft was too narrow for it and it was scraping against the sides. I was nervous anyway at the prospect of the mysterious adventure ahead, and suggested walking upstairs. Paul told me, with a certain malicious amusement, that we couldn't. Part of the staircase above had collapsed, and would probably never get repaired again.

When we stopped at the top floor, the door opposite the elevator flew open with uncanny force and banged loudly against the wall, revealing a dark passageway, lit only by a tiny, red spark within a Moroccan hanging lamp. The effect was strangely intimidating and, no doubt, designed to be. Then, out of the darkness, a big man came striding toward us. He had bold, bright, dark eyes and the kind of sallow skin which looks as if it has been soaked in oil. The eyes were the reverse of 'hypnotic', in the usual journalistic sense; they seemed restlessly inattentive. Anselm (as this obviously was) wore a dirty white terry-cloth bathrobe. On his head was a turban, with a jewel (almost certainly red glass) set in its front. On his fingers were a number of big rings with entwined serpents and other emblems, zodiacal or cabalistic. The trousers of a conventional suit were visible below the bathrobe. On his feet were yellow leather pointed Moroccan slippers. The whole outfit suggested a sort of emergency compromise between

everyday and ritual dress, as when a priest hurriedly
puts on his stole over his street clothes to hear a
dying man's confession.

Anselm bowed to us now with palms pressed together, Hindu style. Then he intoned, 'The Will is
the Law, the Law is the Will; the Great Serpent has
arisen to the Third Lotus and bids you enter.' (I was
suddenly tempted to challenge this mumbo jumbo
and possibly bewilder him by replying with an au-
thentic quotation from the Tantra; but that would
have been spoilsport as well as bad manners.)

As we entered the apartment Anselm switched on
more lights within the hanging lamp, so that the
walls of the passage were better illuminated and I
could see they were hung with pictures. Anselm
signed to Paul to come with him into a room on the
left; I could tell by his manner that I wasn't supposed to follow. As I started to examine the pictures,
I could hear them talking in low voices. The pictures
were crudely but strikingly painted; mostly porno-
graphic and all rather frightening. One was of a bare
stubbly field, across which two men dressed like
Mexican peons were walking. In the foreground, behind a clump of cactus, a ferocious-looking penis
with a fanged shark's mouth and slitty pig's eyes was
lurking ready to rush out and attack them. Another
showed a screaming man being swallowed by an immense grinning vulva with closed eyes on either side
of its opening; this was captioned 'love is blind'. In
another, a young man was standing outside the window of a small house looking at what appeared to
him to be an attractive nude girl. All *he* could see of

her were her head, arms and naked breasts, as she leaned on the window-sill, looking out at him and beckoning him to come inside, with a seductive smile. But the side wall of the house had been removed so that you could see what was invisible to the young man—that the girl's body ended in the tail and rattles of a snake.

At the end of the passage I entered a room which was decorated and furnished in conventional 'mystic' style. The signs of the Zodiac were painted around the walls. There was a crystal on a velvet-draped table, beside a pack of tarot cards. A cheap Buddha, which could have come from any Japanese goods store, stood on a bookcase, with two joss-sticks burning in front of it. In a corner there was a filing-cabinet of the usual grey-painted metal. On its drawers were descriptive cards: *plagues, mantrams, mudras, curses, love-spells, power-words, runes, boons, talismans, miscellaneous mischiefs*. These were printed in large clear lettering and were obviously meant to catch the eye and make a suitable impression on anyone who found himself in the room. 'The man's just a common conjurer,' I said to myself, in disappointment.

At this moment Paul appeared. He drew me over to the window, which, I now noticed, opened on to a balcony.

'Have you got five thousand francs on you, Chris?' he asked, almost in a whisper.

'Why?'

'Because we need it.'

'Why do we need it?'

'Oh, please, now, Chris, be reasonable—don't argue? *You* need it. It's sort of a fee Anselm charges. An initiation fee . . .'

'*Initiation?* Look, what goes *on* here?'

'Keep calm, will you, sweetheart. Didn't you promise your Auntie. . . . ?'

'Okay. Forget it. Here you are. . . .'

I paid out the bills to Paul—remembering how you pay that extra fee to the guide who shows you the 'naughty' frescoes at Pompeii—and he opened a door into a room on the right; a much smaller room, which was nearly bare of furniture. Around it were black velvet mattresses placed end to end. The walls were entirely covered by hangings with intricate Arab designs on them, coloured purple, orange and green.

There were three other people in the room already; a middle-aged woman with henna'd hair, a young Jewish-American girl with a long nose and a very sexy figure, a young Englishman with long thin legs and a certain boyish prettiness. Paul said, 'This is Chris—Prim, Boots, Dexter.' I took a mild dislike to Dexter because of his face and clothes; he was dressed like a bohemian poet of the 'nineties. I had no particular feelings, at first, about either Prim, the woman, or Boots, the girl. And they obviously felt very little interest in me. I sat down on one of the mattresses. It was uncomfortably hard.

Anselm now came in, followed by an Arab youth with a big copper tray on which were various kinds of food. 'Isherwood,' said Anselm, in his deep voice, 'this is Mokhtar, my assistant—or, as some believe, my familiar.'

Mokhtar grinned. He wore Moorish clothes: bag trousers and an open sleeveless jacket which showed parts of his lithe brown body. There was a slyness about him which reminded me of the boys on Ambrose's island. He was evidently very much in control of the situation—whatever the situation was.

'I wonder if you'd prefer to start with kif or majoun?' Anselm said to me. He was polite, but somehow not quite in the right way, like a car-salesman. I analysed his accent as Irish veneered with Old School Tie. I must have looked blank at his question because he added, 'Our Mutual Friend tells me you're a stranger to the subtleties of *cannabis indica?*'

'He means hashish,' Paul told me, 'or, as we backwoods Americans call it, marijuana. Honey, you'd better put yourself in Auntie's hands. . . .' He turned to Mokhtar, 'Let's start him on majourn, because it's so delicious my baby'll just love it!' He slapped the boy familiarly on the buttocks. 'Mokhtar can make majoun do *anything* to you—and I've already explained to him exactly what it is *you* need, Chrissikins. . . . Let's see now, you'd better not drink anything, as this is your first time. While you're eating the majoun, I'll fix you a kif cigarette.'

Paul was right about the majoun being delicious; it looked and tasted rather like Christmas pudding. I ate it with a tiny coffee spoon, while Paul slit open an ordinary American cigarette, mixed kif with the tobacco and rerolled the mixture in a new cigarette-paper. The kif smelled like newly-cut grass in the catcher of a lawn-mower. (Even now, the memory of that smell gives me a very faint sensation of fear.) When Paul had finished doctoring several cigarettes he began drinking a Martini. I asked him if he wasn't going to take any hashish. He shook his head and smiled. 'That stuff doesn't do anything for me now,' he said, like an adult who has outgrown soda-pop.

Anselm, meanwhile, had lighted a long wooden kif-pipe, hung with charms and amulets made of gold, silver and tortoise-shell; he told me he had brought it back with him from the Sahara. Anselm puffed at the pipe, occasionally handing it to Prim, Boots and Dexter, who smoked it in turn while they chatted. Paul made me eat a bowl of mutton stew from the tray, and drink mint tea; these, he said, would help the action of the drug. I smoked two kif cigarettes, inhaling deeply in my eagerness for the intoxication to start. All of a sudden I had lost my fear of it. In this way, I think, about an hour passed. I don't remember saying much, if anything, to Paul. As for the others, I had a definite disinclination to talk to them. Already I was withdrawing into myself.

My symptoms began with seasickness. The room rolled slowly but heavily to starboard, righted itself, rolled to port. I tried to roll with it, forcing what must have been a queasy smile. This wasn't too bad. But now I began to be conscious of the smallness of the room. It was exceedingly small. *And it was getting smaller.* If I stayed here, *it would soon get smaller than I was;* but that was unthinkable. *Out—*

out before it's too late! I got to my feet with perhaps exaggerated casualness. 'You all right, honey chile?' Paul asked.

'No.'

'You mean it's started, already?'

'Sure has.'

'Good.'

I strolled out into the 'mystic' room with the Buddha and the crystal. Paul didn't offer to come to my assistance and I was glad, because I was only just holding on to my self-control. Nobody seemed to take notice of my leaving. I was probably moving fairly normally, though I have an impression that I walked with a high-stepping gait, like a *haute école* horse.

I opened the window and went out on to the balcony, wanting to be as far away as possible from the smallness of the small room. But this was a hideous mistake, as I realized at once. For, out here, the windy, empty, gaping, all-swallowing blackness was too *big* to contain me—much much too big! I must get *out*—out of the outdoors—before I was sucked up into it, and lost for ever. I fled back inside, and peeped cautiously into the smaller room. It was all right now; merely small. I sank back into my place on the mattress with panting relief.

But my relief was very short-lived. And what now followed was worse. It was the beginning of the *slyness; the first of the tricks*. As I lay there with my back against the wall I became aware that there *was no wall*. Oh yes, I was still being supported, but that was irrelevant. I was sitting, as it were, on the sheer edge of Glacier Point, with my back to the three thousand foot precipice and the chasm of all Yosemite yawning one inch behind me. If I turned my head I should see that my support didn't really exist. So I didn't turn my head.

My next problem was the doorway to the room. No—that expressed their relation wrongly. One should say, *the room to the doorway*. The doorway, not the room, was the problem. I called it a doorway, not doorways, because I was still aware that this was really—whatever 'really' meant—a room with only one doorway. What I was now perceiving was an infinite potentiality of doorways, out of which one was being, you might say, 'recognized', as a speaker is 'recognized' by the chairman of a meeting. But *how* and *why* had this particular doorway been chosen? The very thought of having to make such a choice was mental torture. All of the potential doorways were now visibly present, in a tight, endlessly complex and somehow menacing relation to the chosen one. And now, in a flash, I saw what an unspeakably terrifying thing Cubism is. Picasso must have known this, and Braque and Juan Gris. Naturally, they did not talk about it. They did not want to be locked up as madmen. They were the bravest men who have ever lived.

As without, so within. The shifting, sliding planes of potentiality weren't only outside and around me. *I* was potential. *I* was shifting. *I* was no longer in focus as I. The thumbscrew had been touched, ever so slightly, and now all my edges were blurred. One more touch and I should be infinitely nothing. I shut my eyes and held my breath, lest the desperately delicate balance should be upset for ever.

And now, in the next room, Anselm had started a phonograph playing some popular records. Their words, he told us, were Hungarian; but they must have been directly translated from French cabaret songs, for they had exactly the same breathless archness and *oo-la-la!* These records were exquisitely painful to my nerves. I felt literally trapped within the limits of their strict triviality. I paced these limits like a caged animal. I looked around me in desperation for some relief, with the result that my eyes got trapped too, within the Arab designs on the wall-hangings. I couldn't get my eyes out of the design or my ears out of the music. The limits of the music and the limits of the design were parts of the same cage!

But the songs were painful to me for another reason; they were in a foreign language. Ordinarily, this would have enabled me to ignore them altogether. But, in my present state, it was impossible for me to do this; I had not only to listen to them but to try to understand them. And I could! I now found myself possessed of this useless and burdensome psychic power. As long as I listened only to the rhythm of the language—making no attempt to guess at or deduce the meaning of its individual words—I understood it totally, without any question of error. If, however, I said to myself 'that's Hungarian', then at once I ceased to understand. I kept doing this, because I didn't *want* to understand the songs. They meant nothing but their own cruel banality, from which I was straining to escape.

I strained too hard, perhaps; because now my mind began to slip its gears and race and whirr. It was actually running away with me, and I was scared as I had been once when the brakes of my car failed on the steep part of La Cienega Boulevard. Something had to be done instantly. I turned to Paul for help. He wasn't there. I'd had no awareness of his having left the room; but then, I'd had no awareness of any event outside my own area of attention. Dexter was sitting nearest to me, so I hooked my attention on to him; it was like drawing another boat to you with a boathook. And it worked! Gradually, my mind slowed down, the whirring stopped. I felt, with relief, that a new phase of the intoxication was announcing itself. And indeed this *was* the beginning— of the *great horrors!*

Dexter seemed altogether different from the young man I'd seen on coming into this room. He was utterly revealed to me now; and my mild dislike of him was changed into horror and loathing. There he sat, facing life with a pout of greed; boyishly imperious, capricious, endowed with a certain power to do harm which he exercised petulantly. At life's hotel, his complaint to the manager would be that he was bored. And, for this, someone had got to suffer—by George they had! And, at the same time, he was watching out of the corner of his eye, hoping that a real Adult, a Father-Figure, would notice him and bother to come over and take away the toys he had broken and smack his bottom. That would be his greatest thrill. So far, no one had bothered.

Nevertheless, he wasn't negligible, wasn't pitiful,

wasn't merely a nuisance. He was intensely, actively bad. Astonishingly venomous for his size, like that tiny-mouthed viper you can scarcely see in the dust. Ah, how obscene he was—sipping his cocktail and cutely puffing at his kif and telling old red-headed Prim, 'Let's face it, dear, she's nothing but a crashing bore, since she went blind. . . .' The innermost accent of evil was in the sentence. I saw his jaw harden as he pronounced the words; it was the clacking wooden jaw of a ventriloquist's puppet. 'Silly old bag!' he added, with screaming cockatoo laugh, 'the other day she put her hand *right in the fire,* hunting for a ring she'd dropped!' His jaw wagged, then snapped shut on its string.

But where was the ventriloquist? I looked up. Anselm was standing in the doorway. He must have just turned off the phonograph. Now he clapped his hands. Mokhtar appeared.

The situation was becoming complex. I now had to try to attend to several people at once; and this, in my condition, was nearly impossible. Each redirection of my attention cost me a conscious effort. I did my best.

Mokhtar squatted on the floor and began to play a kind of flute. The thin wailing music that it made had an extraordinary power. Never have I heard any sound so nakedly sexual. It didn't provoke or entice; it *was* Sex. You had to recognize that, even if you didn't want it at the moment. *I* didn't want it; no doubt that was because of the way my majoun had been prepared. Boots *did* want it. She stripped off all her clothes and lay down on her belly on the mat, well within Mokhtar's reach. He merely grinned, however, and went on playing.

And now Anselm started to chant; this was evidently some of the rigmarole he used on his disciples or customers or whatever you could call them. 'Take and it shall be given unto you; rape and ye shall find. Only in the sacrament of shame is virtue to be found. Behold me! I roll in excrements. I enter in by the forbidden aperture. I feast on the uttermost vileness. I make free with the flesh that I require. . . .'

As Anselm reached this point in his chanting, he stooped down over Boots, gripped her shoulder, turned her over on her back and suddenly scratched her with his old yellow claw-nails right across the belly, so hard that they left bloody marks on the skin.

Three things were peculiarly horrible about this scene.

First, the whinny of excitement uttered by Prim. Prim's excitement was horrible, just because it *wasn't* plain old ordinary sadism, that much over-rated horror. Prim wasn't even being fanatical. Her whinny expressed the simple glee of the average non-involved civilian: *goody-goody for our side!* That uncritically adopted team-spirit which moves nice wholesome men and women, millions of them, to accept and applaud lynchings, pogroms, concentration-camps, without bothering to understand what they are all about. Prim was for Anselm, so—*goody-goody!* Anything he chose to do was perfectly all right with her.

Boots' reaction was equally horrible in a different

way. How to describe that smile with which she accepted the scratching? She was no more a masochist than Prim was a sadist. No—what I saw in the way she smiled at Anselm was sheer cynical depravity. She was one of those who let themselves be outraged because, in spite of everything, it is *less trouble* than any kind of resistance or positive response. By their consent, they become the parents of future atrocities.

But if Prim and Boots were horrible, Anselm himself was a hundred times more so. The look on his face as he clawed Boots! As I watched him, I understood that, if a Devil *did* exist, the most terrifying thing about him might be simply this: that he wasn't interested in anything, even in damnation. Anselm didn't for one instant believe in his tarot cards, spells, incantations. He didn't believe in scratching Boots. Then why had he scratched her? *For no reason whatsoever.* As he was doing it, his face had shown no cruelty, no lust; nothing but absence of attention.

And now, suddenly, Anselm, Prim, Boots, Dexter, Mokhtar—all of them—were leaving me. Some of them might have walked out already, some might still be in the room; that made no difference. In either case, like balloons with their strings cut, they were drifting away; and at an immense speed. Or you could put it that the room was expanding immensely; the distance across it could now only be measured in light-years. Now they were all gone. I was alone.

All right then, so I was alone. Was that bad? Why should I mind? What had Augustus taught me? What had I been learning through my own experience all these last years? Did I believe what I claimed to believe, or didn't I?

Yes. I looked for my belief, and yes—here it was, available to me. My experience was true. 'This thing' was with me. I didn't have to move one inch. I was right here where everything was. And would always be. Nothing else mattered. I didn't need other people. I didn't need the room. The room could go. It *was* going, faster and faster. I could no longer see the walls. I didn't need the walls. 'This thing' was all I needed. Only . . . the speed made me dizzy. . . . I shut my eyes. For an instant, I felt a great soaring joy, such as I had never known before. I was soaring toward the joy, and everything but the joy was receding from me. But—not so fast! No—wait—wait for me! I couldn't let myself go so fast. Make it stop! And then I was in a panic, and falling. I tumbled back into the room, opening my eyes.

The room was back to normal, and empty.

They had all gone and left me alone. I wanted them back, even if they were horrible. Anything, rather than being alone. All, all alone. My misery became poignant. I was a little kitten, locked out in the winter snow. A poor helpless tiny thing. I was ready to beg them not to desert me. I didn't care what they thought. I was shameless. I was desperate. . . .

'Paul! Paul! *Where are you?*'

'Right here, honey,' said Paul, appearing at once in the doorway.

'Where have you *been?*'

'Just stretching my legs. I stepped into the other room a minute.'

'A *minute!* You've been gone *for ever!*'

Paul gave me one of his searching, medical looks. It was as if I'd unconsciously revealed something to him. He came over and sat down beside me on the mattress.

'Look at your watch,' he said.

He seemed somehow abnormally real, and even more *visible* than usual; more boldly printed, in stronger colours, on the field of my vision. (No doubt this was because I had dimmed the identity of the others by transforming them into symbolic figures, while Paul had remained simply Paul to me, throughout the evening.)

'Why? Why should I look at my watch?'

'Look at your watch.'

I looked at my watch.

'What time is it?' Paul asked.

'A quarter past two. Why?'

'No—tell me *exactly.*'

'Two seventeen. . . . Why do you want to know?'

Paul didn't answer. I felt the horrors coming on again, very big. This was different from the being alone; worse. It was the bottom of everything. The ice-cold awful opposite of joy. I sat with the back of my head against the wall.

'Paul—what is this place?'

'Don't you know, honey chile?'

We were talking in a quiet, conversational, almost dreamy manner.

'I mean—where *are* we?'

'I know where *I* am. I don't now where you are.'

'Could we be in two different places?'

'Why not?'

'Paul—I'm *scared!*'

'There's nothing to be scared of, baby. Nothing in this world. Let's us two just talk this over quietly, shall we? Only you've *got* to keep calm. Nothing bad'll happen to you as long as you keep calm. So will you promise me to?'

'All right. I promise.'

'That's my boy! And now you tell me, *just for the sake of argument,* why you couldn't be some place else, right here at this moment?'

'But that's impossible! I mean—we're in a flat in a house on a street. It's part of a city, in France. It's marked on maps. It has a name. . . . It can't be two places at once, *can it?* And what about all the people who live in this city? The ordinary people. They'd know about it too. They'd notice something was wrong . . .'

'Not necessarily.'

'Why not?'

'You *really* want me to explain that to you?'

'Of course I do!'

'This is just for the sake of argument, mind. *I'm* not saying where you are or where you aren't. Only *you* can say that.'

'Allright—just for the sake of argument . . .'

'Take a hold on yourself, now. You may not like this.'

'What won't I like?'

'You want me to go ahead?'

'Sure!'

'Okay, then. . . . What time was it when you looked at your watch? No—don't look again! Just tell me.'

'Let's see—two seventeen. . . . But what's that got to do with . . . ?'

'*Now* look at your watch.'

I looked at my watch. There was no difficulty about reading it. My mind and my eyesight seemed perfectly clear. I stared and stared. I couldn't at first believe what I saw. But there was no question whatsoever. It was two-seventeen. *Even the minute-hand hadn't moved.*

'Oh Jesus Christ,' I heard myself saying, quite quietly.

'You see what I mean?' said Paul pleasantly, as though he had scored a point in a purely theoretical discussion. 'You *could* be some place else, right here and now. None of the ordinary people, as you call them, would notice anything. They couldn't possibly. It takes time to notice something—even if it's only an instant. But suppose you're in a place where being there doesn't take any time at all?'

I felt the sweat cold on my forehead. I was starting to shake all over. The times I'd thought I'd been *really* scared—when the plane nearly crashed in Mexico over the mountains, when I waited in the surgeon's office to show him my little tumour—why, they were nothing now, mere trifles, huge fun . . .

'Augustus knows the score all right,' Paul was saying. 'The only mistake he makes is trying to tell other people. You can't. Everyone has to find out for

himself. If you talk about it, it's nothing at all—just
another lousy word. . . .'

'What word?'

'Eternity.'

It was then that I completely lost my head. I got
up and went plunging into the next room, where I
knocked over the table with the crystal. There was
the passage leading to the door of the flat. Archi-
tecturally, it was maybe thirty feet long; psychologi-
cally it was at least a mile. But I had to get to that
door. I had to find a way out of the Arab design on
the wall-hangings; for the design had suddenly *become* the flat itself, and I was trapped in it. I began
running down the passage. I ran and ran and ran. I
gasped for air. My lungs burned. I had a stabbing
pain in my side.

Through an open doorway I caught a glimpse of
Mokhtar, Dexter, Boots and Prim. All of them were
naked, and, under ordinary circumstances, I should
have said that Prim was being raped. That is to say,
she was fighting and yelling, and Boots and Dexter
were holding her down and Mokhtar was behaving
erotically. But the word 'rape' had no meaning now,
because a rape is an act, and an act has a beginning
and an end, and exists in time. There was no time in
this place. And there was no place, either.

Then—quite suddenly—I was at the door. Anselm appeared briefly. He was wearing a heavy
gold-embroidered bishop's cope over his bathrobe.
'The Great Serpent forbids . . .' he began. But already I had got the door open and burst out of the

Arab design, and was frantically pushing the button of the elevator.

Nothing happened. Nothing happened. Nothing happened. My voice had come back now, so I screamed and screamed. Paul came quietly out of the flat and opened the elevator door for me, showing that it had been up on the top floor and waiting, all along. He wanted to ride down with me, but I wouldn't let him. I hit at him to stop him from getting into the elevator. Even in the midst of my hysteria I was aware that he understood how I was feeling and didn't really resent this.

When I got out of the building I ran along the street until I came to lights and a bistro which was open. Here, I summoned up the courage to look at my watch. Time had started up again—but in bottom gear, it seemed. For my escape had taken less than five minutes.

The worst was over now. But when I got back to my hotel room and into bed I found I was afraid to switch the lamp off.

Section III | *Limitations*

Hallucinatory Constants

Mescaline has been of unusual interest because of its remarkable psychological and physiological effects. Particularly the visual effects have been the subject of many studies. Viet and Vogt injected various alkaloids, including mescaline, into animals, which were then killed to determine the concentration of the poison in different parts of the central nervous system and in other tissues. The amount of mescaline recovered from the occipital cortex of monkeys and dogs did not differ significantly from that found in the frontal cortex. As regards the effects on the optical sensorium, Maloney claimed that injections of mescaline sulfate led to an enormous enlargement of visual fields in "blind or nearly blind" tabetics and to an improvement in visual acuity, as measured by Snellen's test types. Some of the patients were enabled to read who, previous to the injection, could not; one of them went to a motion-picture show. Recently Zádor reported that mescaline restored perception of movement in the hemianopic field of one of his patients. In this connection, the appearance of the "reddish-blue arcs" of the retina in the mescalinized state is of interest. It is generally agreed that these elliptical reddish-blue arcs, discovered by Purkinje, correspond to fibers of the optic nerve, which become entoptically visible. Normally, these arcs are very distinct for only a moment, but after an injection of mescaline sulfate the author noticed that they could be seen for a long time.

It is characteristic of the action of many drugs that visual effects predominate. Dominance of visual phenomena, a *traduzione visiva* (Sante de Sanctis), seems to be also typical of deliriums, dreams, and eidetic imagery. As regards the hallucinatory phenomena produced by mescaline, their chief character, according to Havelock Ellis, is their "indescribableness." More than a decade ago, the author raised the question whether it was possible to find any constants in the flow of these "indescribable" experiences and analyzed the available data with reference to the *form* of the hallucinatory material. Investigators, such as Berze, emphasizing the importance of motor, kinesthetic, or "myopsychic" components in hallucinations, have called attention to the fact that most visual hallucinations are *formed*. There is no doubt that most reports on hallucinations refer to forms of some kind and not to the appearance of visual "dust" or similar material.

The author's analysis of the hallucinatory phenomena appearing chiefly during the first stages of mescaline intoxication yielded the following *form constants:* (a) grating, lattice, fretwork, filigree, honeycomb, or chessboard; (b) cobweb; (c) tunnel, funnel, alley, cone, or vessel; (d) spiral. Many phenomena are, on close examination, nothing but modifications and transformations of these basic forms. The tendency towards "geometrization," as expressed in these form constants, is also apparent in the following two ways: (*a*) the forms are frequently repeated, combined, or elaborated into ornamental designs and mosaics of various kinds; (*b*) the elements constituting these forms, such as the squares in a chessboard design, often have boundaries consisting of geometric forms. At times, the boundaries are represented by lines so thin that it may be impossible to say whether they are black or white. Many observers have stressed the fineness of these lines, especially Ceroni and Moller. As Moller has pointed out, the "absolute one-dimensional" appears to have become a reality.

For the sake of analysis in terms of "form," we have ignored aspects of color, brightness, and movement, but it is just these aspects which often deeply impress the subject and which he cannot adequately characterize when describing the kaleidoscopic play of forms and patterns. He may, for instance, claim that colors unknown in his previous experience appear; he may even be more impressed by the textures of colors—"fibrous, woven, polished, glowing, dull, veined, semi-transparent"; he may insist that the hallucinatory objects consist of materials that are never seen in nature and yet may strangely resemble certain kinds of wood, straw, hair, jewels, wool, silk, or marble. If we ignore the colors and movements as well as the "meaning" with which the phenomena are invested by the subject, the geometric-ornamental structure of the hallucinations becomes apparent. This appears even in the drawings made by artists during or after mescaline intoxication. Such drawings have been published by Szuman, Marinesco, and Maclay and Guttmann.

The fact that certain geometric forms and designs constantly recur has led us to assume certain hallucinatory form constants. Although further analysis may reveal additional form constants, it seems certain that the number of basic forms is limited. At certain stages of the poisoning, the geometric forms and designs may be seen with open as well as with closed eyes, e.g., on the face of a person or on the soup the subject is about to eat. It is significant that the tendency toward these forms may be so strong as to dominate the perception of external objects. One of Beringer's subjects looked at the small branch of a tree and reported: "The leaves . . . suddenly appeared in an ornamental pattern as if joined in a circular design having the form of approximately a cobweb. I looked at other branches, and, looking at them, all leaves assumed the same lattice-like arrangement."

Some or all of the form constants found in mescaline hallucinations are also found in certain hypnagogic hallucinations, in entoptic phenomena, in the visual phenomena of insulin hypoglycemia, and in phenomena induced by simply looking at disks with black, white, or colored sectors rotating at certain speeds. Occasionally they seem even to occur in fever deliriums. One of the patients of Wolff and Curran, who happened to be a trained observer and physician, reported that he observed the same hallucinatory phenomenon during four illnesses precipitated by four different agents (measles, malaria, tonsillitis, influenza) at the ages of 8, 12, 30, and 41: he saw a cloud "with a spiral motion shape itself into a brilliant whorl." In two of these illnesses he saw that "Brilliantly illuminated green, yellow and red angular crystalline masses shaped themselves into ever-changing patterns like those formed by bits of glass in a revolving kaleidoscope." It can be easily seen from the descriptions and drawings furnished by Purkinje that all the geometric forms and designs characteristic of mescaline-induced phenomena can, under proper conditions, be entoptically observed.

Let us consider, for instance, the form constant for which "funnel," "tunnel," "cone," or similar descriptive terms are used. This form occurs again and again in mescaline hallucinations; it also appears in hypnagogic hallucinations, in entoptic phenomena, and in the phenomena arising when flickering fields are viewed under certain conditions. Or let us consider the "honeycomb" design consisting of hexagons. Purkinje and a number of other observers saw hexagonal patterns entoptically. After awakening in the morning, König frequently noticed, with eyes closed, that his whole visual field was filled up with hexagons (as in a honeycomb). The author saw after awakening, on two different occasions, a pattern almost identical with König's but saw it on the ceiling and not with closed eyes. One of Klien's patients frequently saw, with eyes open, a hexagonal network during migraine attacks. Weil reported that he saw König's design when observing visual phenomena in the hypoglycemic state. The subjects of Haack saw hexagonal patterns when viewing flickering fields. It is clear, therefore, that the honeycomb design, with its hexagonal elements, appears not only in the hallucinatory phenomena produced by mescaline but also under many other conditions. The same is true with respect to the other form constants.

In an "enquiry into the causes of mescal visions," Marshall has tried to show that the form constants proposed by the author can arise only from some peripheral stimulation that is common to different persons. He accounts for the different form constants by reference to various structures within the eye. It is of special interest that among these he includes retro-retinal structures and the choriocapillary circulation. He concludes from anatomical, physiological, and observational data of various kinds that "the rods and foveal cones can look backwards" and that the retinal pigment and the choriocapillary circulation can, therefore, be seen under certain conditions. Similarly, physiologists have attempted to account for entoptic phenomena in general by connecting them with secretions on the cornea, moving particles in the vitreous humor, the network of retinal vessels, the properties and states of the cornea, lens, or other intraocular structures.

Hoppe, one of the chief exponents of a peripheral theory of visual hallucinations, maintained as early as 1887 that "central (direct, immediate, psychic) hallucinations" arising somewhere in the brain do not exist and that "the entoptic content of the eye" always furnishes the "hallucinatory material." Morgenthaler and others have emphasized peripheral factors even in the hallucinations of dementia praecox patients. Zucker injected mescaline into patients who had hallucinations. As a result of these injections, the tapestry design and modifications of the chessboard design appeared, among other hallucinatory phenomena, in some of his schizophrenic patients. Zádor's patients with tract hemianopia (amaurosis of one eye, blindness in temporal region of other eye) saw, under the influence of mescaline, kaleidoscopic phenomena, squares, and other geometric figures in the whole visual field before both eyes. A totally blind patient (amaurosis due to tabes) frequently reported seeing a beautiful chessboard design in the mescalinized state, but he also saw a blue pattern with regularly distributed white points when he was not under the influence of the drug. Mescaline did not induce any visual phenomena in a 23-year-old patient whose eyes had been enucleated during the second year of life.

It must be said that the experiments on patients with some pathology of the visual system leave so many points unsettled that no general conclusions are warranted. The visual effects, as well as the conditions under which they have been obtained, are often so incompletely described that even available data cannot be interpreted. As Guttmann has pointed out, the crucial experiment with congenitally blind persons still remains to be done. It is a well-

known fact that blind persons often report subjective
visual phenomena, such as scintillation or photopsiae like "flames" or "sparks," but sometimes they
also report definite forms and figures. Whether these
figures ever show the patterning indicated in the various form constants described has not yet been systematically investigated. Clear-cut results as to the
form constants present in the visual experiences of
persons with loss of both eyes or totally blind for
other reasons, examined at different intervals after
the onset of blindness, are not available.

One of the author's blind subjects (enucleation of
left eye, glaucoma of right eye) saw "balls with oval
shape," either still or moving, appearing before him
at a distance of about 5 feet. The balls were about
as large as a dime and were only occasionally colored, chiefly red or violet. He also reported seeing
"silver bars," "arabesques," "rings into which you
can put your finger," and "shiny test tubes." He
claimed that the phenomena were more prominent
before his left eye, which had been removed 1½ years
ago, and that they did not appear at all on certain
days. It was impossible to elicit more definite information. Alternating current did not influence or ban-
ish these phenomena. The flicker phenomena that
are seen by normal subjects under certain conditions
of stimulation with alternating current could not be
electrically produced in this subject.

It should be mentioned that the form constants
that we have discussed are apparently not typical for
the visual phenomena produced by electrical stimulation of the occipital lobe in man. Urban found that

the photopsiae consisted mostly of glowing and colored "roundish forms, disks, or rings" when faradic current was used, and of stars and ragged forms such as "pointed sparks" when galvanic current was used.

It should be obvious that the factors determining the appearance of certain form constants are so numerous that all theories stressing either "peripheral" or "central" factors are too simple. That there is an interaction of these factors may be true, but this remains in the present state of our knowledge a vague assertion. We wish to stress merely one point, namely, that under diverse conditions the visual system responds in terms of a limited number of form constants. Any general theory, however, will have to go beyond a consideration of visual mechanisms per se. The mescaline-produced phenomena demonstrate this point in a striking manner. Mescaline induces changes not only in the visual field but also in other sensory spheres, particularly in the somatosensory sphere. "Haptic hallucinations" and other somatosensory phenomena may dominate the symptomatology to the exclusion of phenomena in the visual sphere.

We shall not enter into a description of the somatosensory changes, but merely mention that Professor Forster, for example, felt a net similar to a "cobweb" on his tongue: "When I opened my mouth, a cold wind passed through and the net moved." Serko frequently had the sensation that his legs or his feet consisted of "spirals." In his case, sometimes the haptic spiral of a leg blended with a luminous spiral that had been rotating in the visual field. "One has the sensation of somatic and optic unity." To dismiss such phenomena as synesthetic experiences merely emphasizes the present lack of knowledge concerning the processes involved in synesthesias and intersensory relations in general. A physician, a subject of Beringer, "saw" and "felt" the sounds of a concertina played by the experimenter, and the pain produced by it coagulated as luminous curves in the spiral turns of his body, the lower part of his body being a green varnished cone with spiral windings. Such experiences would probably be classified as instances of complex synesthesias. However, a form constant may involve so many spheres that even a synesthetic basis would be too narrow. In one of Beringer's subjects (also a physician), the "lattice" or "fretwork" constant became so dominant that it appeared to penetrate the whole personality.

The subject stated that he saw fretwork before his eyes, that his arms, hands, and fingers turned into fretwork and that he became identical with the fretwork. There was no difference between the fretwork and himself, between inside and outside. All objects in the room and the walls changed into fretwork and thus became identical with him. While writing, the words turned into fretwork and there was, therefore, an identity of fretwork and handwriting. "The fretwork is I." All ideas turned into glass fretwork, which he saw, thought, and felt. He also felt, saw, tasted, and smelled tones that became fretwork. He himself was the tone. On the day following the experiment, there was

Nissl (whom he had known in 1914) sitting somewhere in the air, and Nissl was fretwork. "I saw him, I felt him; Nissl was I."

It seems necessary to assume some basic process operative in different sense modalities to cope with all varieties of synesthetic experiences. Even the fact that a sensory impression or a hallucination in one of the sense fields is followed by manifestations in other sense fields does not give us the right to speak of "primary" and "secondary" sensations (or hallucinations) except in the sense of a temporal succession. One event may be primary and another one secondary in this sense, and yet the intersensory relation may involve only one basic process. Similarly, we may doubt whether the preceding example of a "mescal psychosis" with "fretwork" or "lattice" as the central theme can be understood by considering the hallucinatory occurrence of the fretwork in the visual field as the "primary" event that determines "secondary" and "tertiary," etc., events, such as changes in other sense fields and in the mechanisms of thought and emotion.

In a further search for hallucinatory constants, we shall again start with a consideration of the form factor. We note that a single form (figure, object) may be duplicated or multiplied, that its size may change or that its shape may be altered or distorted; i.e., we may have monocular or binocular diplopia or polyopia; dysmegalopsia (micropsia or macropsia); metamorphopsia or dysmorphopsia.

If we analyze the visual phenomena produced by

mescaline, we find diplopia, polyopia, dysmegalopsia, and dysmorphopsia not only of hallucinatory
objects but also of real or imaginal objects. That is
to say, the same mechanisms may be operative, no
matter whether an object is perceived, imagined, or
hallucinated. The mescaline experiments demonstrate, therefore, that we must go beyond the level of
visual hallucinations to determine hallucinatory constants. In fact, we must even go beyond the visual
mechanisms that cut across distinctions between perception, imagery, and hallucination and raise the
question whether similar mechanisms are operative
in nonvisual spheres. There is no doubt that polyopia, dysmegalopsia, and dysmorphopsia find their
parallel in experiences in the somatosensory sphere.
Subjects in the mescalinized state feel that their
limbs shrink or grow, that they are shortened or
elongated, or that they are distorted in many ways.
The experience of changes in size and the sensation
of distortions and alterations may involve the whole
body. As regards polyopia, its counterpart is found,
for example, in a "polymelia" of the fingers or of the
arms. The subject may feel several arms growing out
of his shoulder until he feels "like the Buddhas." At
times, the alterations in the somatosensory sphere
may be so profound that parts of the body feel separated from the rest. As Serko insisted, there may be
not a "sensation" but a "somatopsychic hallucination" of two bodily forms, e.g. of an amputated leg
and of a foot entirely separate lying beside it.

The tendency toward reduplication appears not
only in polyopia and "polymelia" but also in halluci-

natory experiences involving the presence of one or many persons in the room. Although these persons are not seen, their reality is in some way experienced or "felt." In this connection, it is of interest that "splitting" of personality and various degrees of "depersonalization" have been frequently reported. It may be said, therefore, that polyopia, dysmegalopsia, and dysmorphopsia involve mechanisms that are characteristic of mescaline-induced phenomena not only in the visual sphere (hallucination, imagery, perception) but also in the somatosensory sphere.

Further analysis reveals the fact that mescaline is only one of many agents bringing about polyopia, dysmegalopsia, and dysmorphopsia. Thus, under certain conditions, the sane effects can be observed in "psychogenic" and "nonpsychogenic" hallucinations, even in the *hallucinations autoscopiques*, in the perception of real objects, in visual imagery, in dreams, in eidetic imagery, in hypnagogic hallucinations, in the phenomena that arise when flickering fields are viewed. In other words, reduplication or changes in size or shape of a given visual form may occur, no matter whether the object in question is real or has appeared as the result of looking for a considerable time at a flickering field; whether it is hallucinated, visually imagined, or seen as an eidetic or hypnagogic image. In fact, some spontaneous drawings seem to exhibit similar tendencies, so that Maclay, Guttmann, and Mayer-Gross speak of a "mescaline type" of drawing. By way of summary, it may be said that polyopia, dysmegalopsia, and dysmorphopsia occur not only in visual hallucinations but also in many other phenomena of the visual sphere (visual perception, eidetic imagery, dreams, etc.).

The fact that diverse visual phenomena commonly assigned to different functional levels of the visual system may show the same typical behavior becomes of still greater interest if we consider the various conditions and clinical states in which such typical behavior occurs. The "symptoms" of polyopia, dysmegalopsia, and dysmorphopsia have been observed in different psychoses, especially in toxic psychoses or at the beginning of certain psychoses, in deliriums, in insulin hypoglycemia, in hysteria, in patients with cerebral lesions, particularly with parieto-occipital or occipital lesions, in the basedoid constitution, in eidetic individuals, and in poisonings produced by certain drugs (hashish, cocaine, etc., chronically used). Beringer has called attention to the existence of these symptoms in the acute phases of schizophrenia. The symptoms were especially striking in one of his hebephrenic patients. Gurewitsch has described an "interparietal syndrome" in which polyopia, dysmegalopsia, and dysmorphopsia are combined with alterations in the postural model of the body or in the bodily schema. According to him, this syndrome is found in nosologically different diseases, such as *lues cerebri,* epilepsy, schizophrenia, hysteria, and cerebral trauma. Thus, the optical symptoms are paralleled in the somatopsychic sphere in other conditions as well as in mescaline intoxication.

In trying to account for polyopia, dysmegalopsia, and dysmorphopsia, ophthalmologists have stressed the importance of dioptric and retinal conditions. Such conditions, however, are not likely to explain the occurrence of similar visual changes in imaginal objects or the fact that the alterations selectively affect only specific objects in a room or only parts of certain objects. Since the optical symptoms occur under many different conditions and in diseases with different etiology, the relative importance of the various factors influencing the visual mechanisms may be expected to vary in different conditions or from one disease to the other. However, we should not necessarily expect entirely different factors to become operative if polyopia and related symptoms appear in a schizophrenic, a mescalinized or eidetic individual or in a patient with a parieto-occipital lesion. The search for some basic factor underlying the optical symptoms in etiologically different conditions is undoubtedly surrounded by the same difficulties as the search for so-called neurological syndromes in psychoses. The "interparietal syndrome" of Gurewitsch is present, for instance, not only in patients with cerebral lesions but also in schizophrenic patients in whom such lesions are absent. It would be rash to conclude that the same syndrome is produced by two different agents. Unfortunately, we are far from knowing the pathophysiological mechanisms that become operative as the result of a parieto-occipital lesion. Once the nature of these mechanisms is known, we shall perhaps understand why the same symptoms may appear, for instance, in schizophrenic patients.

The diversity of conditions in which polyopia,

dysmegalopsia, and dysmorphopsia occur has not deterred investigators from looking for some fundamental mechanism. That such a mechanism must be assumed is strongly suggested by the fact that polyopia and related symptoms are characteristic not only of different functional levels in the visual sphere (perception, imagery, hallucination, etc.) but also of the somatosensory sphere. In recent years, the analysis of these symptoms has led most investigators to assign a fundamental role to vestibular factors. It is thought that reduplication of objects, micropsia, macropsia, and dysmorphopsia in hallucinations are indicative of a vestibular influence. The same conclusion is reached, for example, by Menninger-Lerchenthal in his thoroughgoing analysis of autoscopic hallucinations. His view is that autoscopy is a hallucination of the bodily schema which has a visual and a tactile-kinesthetic component. He believes that it does not make any difference whether the study of autoscopic hallucinations is approached from the phenomenological angle or from facts of brain physiology, since the analysis always leads to vestibular factors. Skworzoff has presented similar views. Other investigators have emphasized tonic, postural, and oculomotor factors. In this connection, it is of interest that Potzl and Urban have stressed the importance of the supravestibular system (in the sense of Muskens).

The experimental data on the influence of the vestibular apparatus on the visual sphere are rather meager. Most of the experiments have been concerned with determining the effects of various forms of labyrinthine stimulation (rotation, galvanic, or caloric stimulation) on different visual phenomena. There is no doubt, however, that the available anatomical, clinical, and experimental data are sufficient for supporting the view that any future research directed toward elucidating the role of the vestibular system is bound to yield extremely significant results not only for the study of hallucinations but also, as some neurologists and psychiatrists insist, for a deeper understanding of neurotic and psychotic behavior. It has even been maintained, particularly by French neurologists, that great strides will be made in psychiatry by obtaining data on vestibular chronaxy.

At this point, it is not possible to outline the various experimental problems that urgently require a solution. We shall be content with calling attention to a new technique that may be employed in analyzing different factors influencing hallucinations or other subjective visual phenomena. By applying alternating current of low intensity and frequency, it is possible to produce flicker that is visible with open or closed eyes under conditions of light as well as dark adaptation. During recent years, the author has obtained some data on the behavior of negative afterimages, eidetic images, and hallucinations in the presence of electrically produced flicker. For evaluating the flicker phenomenon itself, it was necessary to examine patients with some pathology of the visual system (hemianopia, enucleation of one eye, etc.). In general negative after-images disappear almost entirely or change radically in appearance the moment the stimulating current is turned on. Cessation of electrical stimulation immediately leads to a reappearance of the after-image and to a restoration of its normal properties. Eidetic images and certain types of hallucinations may vanish, change, or remain unaltered upon appearance of the electrically produced flicker.

To illustrate: one subject, a student, saw an eidetic image of the face of a person looking at him. When the current was turned on, he suddenly saw the profiles of five faces looking to the right. These faces rapidly changed into other faces; they were seen through the "muslin curtain" of the flicker, as the subject expressed it. More than three decades ago, Urbantschitsch used galvanic current for influencing eidetic images. He reports, e.g., that one of his subjects saw an eidetic image of a hepatica. Application of the galvanic current immediately led to the appearance of a large number of hepaticas. It should be realized, of course, that rotation of the subject or electrical and other forms of stimulation may merely accentuate tendencies inherent in eidetic imagery and other subjective phenomena, since polyopia and related visual changes frequently occur in the absence of any stimulation.

To sum up, in our search for hallucinatory constants we have found (*a*) that the reduplication of objects and the alterations in size and form occurring in hallucinations occur also in other visual phenomena and in phenomena of the somatosensory sphere; (*b*) that these symptoms appear under many different conditions and in diseases of different etiology. The involvement of different senses and the occurrence of these symptoms in etiologically different conditions suggest that we are dealing with some fundamental mechanisms involving various levels of the nervous system. To elucidate these mechanisms, we must rely on future research to provide the necessary anatomical, pathological, biochemical, and clinical data. Some investigators have advanced the view that tendencies toward reduplication of objects and toward seeing or feeling objects "enormously large" or "very small" or distorted in certain ways satisfy certain intellectual or emotional needs. Let us assume that there is a desire to reduce a dignified person to Lilliputian dimensions "because he will look so funny." The desire itself is likely to be ineffective in producing micropsia unless it is coupled with a basedoid constitution, some disease process, or some other condition that throws certain neural mechanisms into gear. In fact, emotional or intellectual needs of such a kind, if they should exist, may be merely another expression of the existence of such mechanisms. At any rate, there is an interdependence of many different factors.

A further point should be emphasized. We may say that under normal and pathological conditions certain mechanisms are available for producing a limited number of fundamental alterations in a visual object. Such alterations manifest themselves in polyopia, dysmegalopsia, and dysmorphopsia. But the fact that an alteration, e.g., in shape, occurs as one of a limited number of fundamental alterations does not mean that there is any constancy in the sense that particular shapes or distortions are invariably produced. It seems as though there were no limit to the number of different shapes an object may assume in the visual experiences of different subjects. Every conceivable distortion has been reported. The situation is similar with regard to alterations in size or number of objects. A few fundamental alterations may, therefore, produce phenomenologically a very complex picture, especially since changes in number, size, and shape of objects may combine in many ways. Furthermore, all these changes may occur within the framework of altered spatio-temporal relations. For example, the perception of movement may be radically changed or even become impossible; all objects may appear at the same distance, or they may recede into space without changing size (porrhopsia).

In determining hallucinatory constants, we have so far been primarily concerned with the properties or changes of single objects and configurations. Our next step is to consider the behavior of these objects in space and the relation of objects to each other. We shall start from certain facts obtained in experimental investigations of eidetic imagery.

In studying the behavior of certain types of eidetic imagery, we find an occurrence of the following changes: there is a translocation of objects or parts of objects; parts or properties of one object are transferred to another object; only fragments or certain parts of an object appear; the appearance of one object is accompanied by the disappearance of another; an object undergoes rotational displacements

of various kinds (mirror reversals, etc.); there occurs a splitting up of objects into many fragments;
objects appear that did not constitute parts of the
preceding stimulus situation; a given object
disappears and reappears periodically; objects or
parts of objects are entirely missing; objects that appeared in the stimulus situation are missing but appear after relatively long periods of time, even after
hours, in the eidetic image of some other stimulus
situation. The changes just described are characteristic of eidetic images produced by previous stimulation, e.g., by letting the subject view a picture for a
certain length of time. But it should be remarked
that changes occurring in spontaneous eidetic images are often similar in nature.

It is perhaps safe to assume that these changes involve some basic mechanisms, since similar changes
in spatio-temporal relations have been found to
occur in visual agnosia. The fact that the visual perception of patients with traumatic lesions of the occipital lobes should exhibit the same type of spatio-
temporal changes as certain eidetic images is, as
Schilder puts it, "exceedingly surprising" to anybody
familiar with the facts of brain pathology. Pötzl has
called attention to the fact that even the perceptions
of normal persons may show similar changes under
conditions of peripheral vision and in tachistoscopic
experiments. It is of special interest in this connection that Pötzl was able to produce visual hallucinations by tachistoscopic exposures of pictures or
objects in a patient with latent hemianopia and an
alcoholic hallucinosis. The experimentally produced

hallucinations were characterized by changes of the kind found in eidetic imagery. It is apparent that similar changes are characteristic of dreams. In brief, under certain conditions, the same structure of spatio-temporal transformations becomes apparent in eidetic imagery, hallucinations, dreams, and visual perception.

In an attempt to define hallucinatory constants, we have purposely taken visual forms and their interrelations as a point of departure. It is obvious that we have ignored many aspects of hallucinatory phenomena in order to arrive at these constants. *The hallucinatory constants that we have found may be tentatively assigned to three levels: (a) the level of "form constants"; (b) the level of alterations in number, size, and shape (polyopia, dysmegalopsia, dysmorphopsia); (c) the level of changes in spatio-temporal relations.* We have shown that the same constants appear in other visual, and even in nonvisual, phenomena. These constants are, therefore, not specific for hallucinations but represent general characteristics. The "structure" of hallucinations is a general structure that is typical of numberous phenomena in the visual sphere.

7. CHARLES BAUDELAIRE

The Theatre of Seraphim

What does one experience? What does one see?
Things marvellous, things extraordinary? Is this
wonderful and terrible and really dangerous? Such
are the ordinary questions that the ignorant address,
with a curiosity mixed with conceit, to the adepts.
One might say a childish impatience of knowledge,
such as that of those who have never left the corner
of their fires, when they find themselves face to face
with a man who returns from distant and unknown
lands. They figure to themselves the intoxication of
Haschisch as if it were a prodigious prodigality, a
vast theatre of prestidigitation and of jugglery, where
all is miraculous and unexpected. That is a preju-
dice, a complete mistake. And, since for the greater
part of readers and of questioners, the word Haschisch gives them the idea of a strange and over-
thrown world, and the desire of prodigious dreams
(it might be better to say hallucinations, which are
besides less frequent than we suppose), I shall now
remark on the important differences which separate
the effects of Haschisch from the effects of sleep. In
sleep, this adventurous voyage of every night, there
is something positively miraculous; it is a miracle

whose punctuality has baffled mystery. Men's dreams are divided in two classes. Some, full of his ordinary life, of his preoccupations, of his desires, of his vices, are combined in a fashion more or less bizarre with the objects seen during the day, that are indiscriminately fixed on the vast canvas of his memory. That is the natural dream: it is the man himself. But the other kind of dream! the dream absurd, unexpected, without any relation with his character, with his life, with his passions as a dreamer! This dream, that I shall call hieroglyphical, represents evidently the supernatural side of his life, and it is justly so because it is absurd that the ancients believed it to be divine. As it is inexplicable by natural causes, they have attributed to it a cause exterior to the man; and even to-day, without speaking of the Dream Interpreters, there exists a philosophical school which sees in dreams of this kind now a reproach, now an advice; in one word, a pitiless moral and symbolical picture, engendered in the spirit of the man who sleeps. It is a dictionary that he ought to study, a language of which only the Wise can obtain the key.

In the intoxication of Haschisch, nothing of the kind. Our dreams are natural; our intoxication, however long may be its duration, cannot be, is not, really, more than an immense dream, thanks to the intensity of the colours and to the rapidity of conception; but it must always keep the particular tonality of the individual. Man has desired to dream, the dream must govern the man; but this dream will soon be the son of its father. An idle man uses his ingenuity so as to introduce artificially what is super-natural in his life and in his thought; but he is not, after all and despite the accidental energy of his sensations, more than the same man augmented, the same number elevated to an enormous height. He is subjugated; but, for his sins, he is not subjugated except by himself, that is to say by what is dominant in his nature; *il a voulu faire l'ange, il est devenu une bête,* momentarily very powerful, if always he can call power an excessive sensibility, without government for moderating or for exploiting it.

Let men of the world and those who are ignorant, seriously anxious to find the secret of exceptional enjoyments, know to a certainty that they will not find in Haschisch anything miraculous, absolutely nothing but what is naturally excessive. The brain and the organism on which Haschisch operates, give only their ordinary phenomena, individual, augmented, certainly, as to number and energy, but always faithful to their origin. Man cannot escape the fatality of his physical and moral temperament: Haschisch will be, for the man's familiar thoughts and impressions, a deceptive mirror and a pure mirror.

Here is the drug before his eyes: a little green jam, as big as a nut, singularly odorous, to such a point that it sickens the stomach and gives one a nausea, which any fine and agreeable odour might give him, were it heightened to its maximum of force and of destiny. Let me be allowed to observe that this proposition could perhaps be inverted, and that the most repugnant, the most revolting perfumes, might perhaps become pleasant, if they were reduced to their minimum of quantity and of expression. Imagine your happiness! It is contained in the capacity of a small table spoon! Happiness with all its intoxications, all its follies, all its absurdities! You can swallow it without fear: one does not die of it. Your physical organs will receive from it no injury. Later on perhaps a more frequent appeal to the sorcery might diminish the force of your will, perhaps you will be less of a man than you are to-day; but the punishment is so far off, and the future disaster of a nature so difficult to define! What do you risk? To-morrow a little nervous fatigue. Do you not risk every day greater punishments for less recompenses? Thus, it is said: You have yourself, to give yourself more expansion and force, diluted your dose of poison in a cup of black coffee; you have been careful to have an empty stomach, putting off till nine or ten o'clock your dinner, so as to let the poison act; in an hour from now you must take some soup. You are now sufficiently ballasted for a long and singular voyage. You hear the shriek of the steam, the sails are hoisted, and you have over ordinary travellers the curious ignorance of not knowing where you are going. You have desired it, fatally!

I presume that you have taken the precaution of choosing your moment for this expensive expedition. Every perfect Debauch has need of a perfect leisure. You know besides that Haschisch excites not only the exaggeration of the individual, but also of circumstances and surroundings; but you have no duties to accomplish that require punctuality and exactitude; no domestic cares; no love-pangs. You must be very careful of yourself. This chagrin, this disquietude, this memory of something that insists on your using your will and your attention at a given moment, shall soon sound like a death-knell against your intoxication, and shall poison your pleasure. Disquietude will change to anguish; chagrin to torture. If all these preliminary conditions are observed, the weather wonderful, and you yourself in a favourable situation, such as a picturesque landscape or a room artistically decorated, if you can hope to hear some music, then all's for the best.

There are generally three stages in the intoxication of Haschisch easy enough to distinguish, and this is certainly a curious thing to observe, in those who are unused to it, the first symptoms of the first stage. You have heard of the marvellous effects of Haschisch: your imagination has conceived a particular idea, something like an ideal of intoxication; it remains for you to know if its reality will be decidedly at the height of your hopes. This is enough to throw you from the beginning into an anxious state, certainly favourable to the conquering and extraordinary humour of the poison. Many of those who are initiated, at the first degree of initiation, complain of what is tedious in the effects; they wait for it with a futile impatience, and if the drug does not act rapidly enough, they give way to the boasting of incredulity which convey a sardonic sense of satisfaction to the Initiates who know all the effects of Haschisch. The first symptoms of an approaching storm appear and multiply themselves in the midst of this incredulity. It is first of all an outrageous hilarity, irresistible, lu-

dicrous, which seizes on you. These motiveless attacks of hilarity, of which you are ashamed, frequently reproduce themselves and they destroy the
intervals of stupor during which you have lost yourselves. The most simple words, the most trivial ideas,
take on bizarre and fantastic shapes; you are astonished not to have imagined before that they are so
simple. Incongruous resemblances and reconcilia-
tions, impossible to foresee, interminable jests,
comical absurdities, rush continually from your
brain. The Demon has invaded you; it is useless to
be refractory against this hilarity, as dolorous as
when a woman tickles you. From time to time you
laugh at yourselves, at your foolishness and at your
folly, and your friends, if you have any, laugh just as
boisterously as you do at your state and at theirs;
but, as they have no malice, you have no rancour.

This hilarity, languishing and poignant, this uneasiness in joy, this insecurity, this sick indecision,
do not usually endure for more than a certain length
of time. Soon the mixture of ideas becomes so vague,
the conducting wires that hold your conceptions so
tense, that only your accomplices can understand
you. And, besides, on this subject and on this side,
no means of verification; perhaps they suppose that
they can comprehend you, then the illusion becomes
a delusion. This frolicsome spirit and these bursts of
laughter, which are like explosions, appear as a veri-
table folly, at least as a maniac's stupidity, to every
man who is not in the same state as you are. At the
same time, wisdom and sagacity, the regularity of
thoughts in these who are not intoxicated, delight

and amuse you, as if they were particular kinds of lunacy. The parts are inverted. One's frigidity drives you to the last limits of Irony. Is not this a mysteriously comical situation, that of a man who jested at himself with an incomprehensible gaiety for one who has not placed himself in the same situation? The madman takes the wise man in pity, and from thence the idea of his superiority begins to dawn on his intellect's horizon. Soon it will change, become greater and burst like a meteor.

I was present at a scene when this hilarity became excessive, the grotesque side of which was unintelligible except for those who understood, at least by the observation of others, the effects of the substances and the enormous difference of diapason that it created between two intelligences supposedly equal. A famous musician, who ignored the various virtues of Haschisch, who perhaps had never heard it spoken of, falls into the midst of a society where several men had taken the drug: these try to make him comprehend the marvellous effects of the poison. At these prodigious proposals, he smiles with grace, like a man who really wants to *pose* for several minutes. His sense is divined suddenly by those spirits the poison has exasperated; and he is hurt by their laughter. These shouts of joy, these puns on words, these changed faces, all this sickly atmosphere, irritate him to such a point that he declares, perhaps sooner than he has intended, *que cette charge d'artistes est mauvaise et que d'ailleurs elle doit être bien fatigante pour ceux quil'ont entreprise.* The comedy of it illumines all these faces as if by lightning. There is an exacerbation of joy. "This joke might be good for you, but not for me," says one. "It ought to have been good for us," replies egoistically one of these intoxicated men. Not knowing if he has an affair with madmen or with men who simulate folly, our man believes that the wisest thing to do is to retire; one of them locks the door. Another, kneeling before him, asks pardon in the name of the society, and declares to him insolently, but with tears, that despite his spiritual infirmity, which perhaps excited a sense of pity, all are penetrated for him with a deep friendship. The musician, resignedly, remains, and he condescends, on our insistent outcries, to play some music. But the sounds of the violin, as they scattered themselves across the room in as it were a new form of contagion, *seized hold on* (the word isn't too strong) now this, now that, intoxicated man. There are rages and sad sighs, sudden sobs, showers of silent tears. The terrified musician stops suddenly, and, going up to one of those whose beatitude makes the biggest noise, asks him if he suffers much and if he can do anything to soothe him. One of these, a *practical man,* proposes lemonade on acids. But the intoxicated man, with ecstatic eyes, gazes on both of them with an ineffable scorn. To think of healing a man sick with too much life, sick with joy!

As one sees by this anecdote, a sense of self counts for much in the sensations caused by Haschisch; a something silent, sensuous, subtle, which comes directly from the nerves. To add to this observation, a man told me of an adventure which had seized him in this state of intoxication, and how he kept an exact consciousness of his sensations, so that I understood perfectly into what grotesque and inextricable embarrassment this difference of diapason and of level, of which I have spoken, had cast him. I don't recall whether the man in question had been at his first or second experience. Had he taken too strong a dose, or had Haschisch produced, without the aid of any apparent cause (which arrives often enough), more vigorous effects? He told me that across his pleasure, this supreme delight of feeling oneself full of life and of believing oneself full of genius, he had suddenly stumbled on a horrible object. After having been amazed by the beauty of his sensations, he had been suddenly overwhelmed by them. He asked himself what might have happened to his intelligence and to his limbs, if this state that he assumed to be a supernatural state, became more and more aggravated, as his nerves became more and more delicate. Through the faculty of increasing the size of objects that the patient's spiritual eye possesses, this fear ought to become an ineffable punishment. "I was," said he, "like a horse carried away by his own speed in the direction of an abyss. In effect, it was a fearful gallop, and my thought, slave of the circumstance, of the accident and of all that might be implied in the word hazard, had taken a turn purely and absolutely rhapsodic. It was too late! I said to myself with endless despair. When this mood of feeling ceased, which seemed to me to endure for an infinite length of time and which perhaps occupies no more than a few minutes, when I imagined I had plunged myself into a state of beatitude which follows on this furious phase, I was overwhelmed with another misery. I remembered that I had been invited to a dinner to meet some serious men. I saw myself there and then in the midst of a wise crowd, where everyone is master of himself, obliged to hide most carefully the state of my mind, under the light of so many lamps. I was certain I should succeed in dissimulating my state of exasperation, yet I felt all the time that my strength of will was about to leave me. I know not by what accident these words in the gospel: "Woe to him through whom scandal arises!" surged into my memory, and as I tried to forget them I repeated them over and over again. My misery (for it was an absolute misery) took on gigantic proportions. I resolved to make an act of energy and to consult a chemist; for I ignored what reactives are, and I wanted to go, mind and body at rest, to the house where I had been invited. But on the threshold of the shop a sudden thought seized me, which arrested me for several instants and made me reflect; for I had seen myself in passing, in the glass of a window, and my face astonished me. This pallor, these retreating lips, these enormous eyes! I must hasten to this chemist, I thought, and for I know not what stupid reason. Add to this, the sentiment of the ridiculous adventure I wanted to avoid, the fear of finding people in the shop. But my apparent interest in this unknown chemist dominated all my other sentiments. I imagined this man to be as sensitive as myself in this ghastly moment, and as I also imagined that his ear and his soul must become like mine, vibrating at the least noise, I resolved to enter the shop on my lifted heels. I shall not know (I thought) what discretion I shall have to show him—for I want to alarm his charity. I promised myself I would deaden the sound of my voice and the noise of my feet; you know it, this voice of Haschisch? Grave, profound, guttural, not unlike those of the opium-eaters. The result was the exact contrary of what I wanted to obtain; for, decided to reassure the chemist, I terrified him. He recognised nothing of this malady, he had never heard of it. At the same time he gazed at me with a defiant curiosity. Did he take me for a madman? a malefactor or a malcontent? Neither this, nor that; but all these absurd ideas traversed my brain. I was obliged to explain to him at great length—with what fatigue!—the nature of the hemp-seed and how I used it, saying over and over again that there was no danger, that he had not —himself—any reason for being alarmed, and that all I wanted was a means of reaction, insisting frequently on the sincere regret I experienced in causing him any trouble. Finally—understand the concentrated humiliation I endured as I uttered these words—he simply asked me to *leave the shop*. Such was the reward of my charity and of my exaggerated good will. I went to my dinner: I scandalised no one. Nor can anyone divine the superhuman efforts I made so as to resemble all the rest of the company. Never shall I forget the tortures of an ultra-poetical intoxication, all but destroyed by an enforced decorum and a sense of duty!"

Though I am naturally drawn to sympathise with all the sorrows born of the imagination, I couldn't help bursting with laughter after he had finished his confession. The man who made it to me has never corrected himself; he continues to derive from the incensed poison the excitement he needs must find outside himself; but as he is a prudent man, a man of the world, he diminishes the doses, which permits him to increase them when he chooses: he will soon perceive the rotten results of his persistence.

I return to the regular development of the intoxication. After the first stage of childish mirth there is a momentary lull. But soon new events produce a sensation of coldness in the extremities (which can become intensely cold) and a great weakness in all the limbs, as in your hands, your head, in all your being, and you feel an embarrassing stupor and stupefaction. Your eyes expand; they are in a sense drawn inward as all the senses are, by an implacable ecstasy. Your face becomes pallid, your lips rigid as if they sucked themselves, with this movement of inhaling which characterises the ambition of a man a prey to sanguinary obsessions, oppressed by vast projects, as his respiration becomes more difficult. The throat is contracted, so to speak; the palate is tormented by a thirst it would be infinitely sweet to satiate if the delights of idleness were not more agreeable and were not opposed by the least derangement of the body. Raucous and deep sighs escape from your breast, as if your ancient body could not support the desires and the activity of your new soul. From time to time, you shudder, and your shudder gives you an involuntary movement, like those nervous jumps which, at the end of a day's work or of a night's storm, pierce one's definite sleep. . . .

It is at this period of intoxication that a rare quality manifests itself, a superior acuteness in all the senses. Smell, sight, hearing, touch, participate equally in this progress. The eyes have the vision of Eternity. The ear perceives almost unseizable sounds in the midst of a vast turmoil. It is then that the hallucinations begin. Exterior objects assume, in succession, singular appearances, they become deformed, transformed. Then, arrives what is equivocal, such as scorn and the transpositions of ideas. Sounds assume colours and colours contain music. This, one might say, is quite natural, and that any poetical brain, in its sane and normal state, easily conceives these analogies. But I have already warned the reader that there is nothing purely supernatural in the intoxication of Haschisch; only, these analogies assume an unusual vivacity; they penetrate, they invade, they weigh down the spirit with their despotic character. Musical notes become numbers, and if your spirit is gifted with some musical aptitude, melody, heard melody, while it preserves its voluptuous and sensual character, transforms itself into a vast arithmetical operation, when numbers beget numbers, of which you follow the phases and the generation with an inexplicable rapidity and an agility equal to that of the executant.

It often happens that the personality disappears and that the objectivity, which is the proper domain of Pantheistic Poets, develops itself in you so abnormally, that the contemplation of exterior objects makes you forget your own existence, and makes you confound yours with theirs. Suppose you look on a tree waved by the wind; in a few seconds, what was in the brain of a Poet no more than a natural comparison becomes in yours a reality. First you attribute to the tree your passions, your desire and your melancholy; its sobs and oscillations become yours, and before long you are the tree. In the same sense, the bird who flies to the height of the skies *represents* first the immortal desire of flying above things human; already you are yourself the bird. I suppose you seated and smoking. Your attention will find rest in the bluish clouds that rise from your pipe. The idea of an evaporation, slow, successive, eternal, seizes your spirit; and you begin to apply this idea to your proper thoughts, to your thinking matter. Through a singular equivocation, by a kind of transposition or by some intellectual *quid pro quo*, you will feel yourself evaporating, and you will attribute to your pipe (in which you feel yourself crouching in one lump on the tobacco) the strange faculty of *smoking yourself* (*l'étrange faculté de vous fumer*).

Luckily, this interminable imagination only endured for a minute, for an interval of lucidity, with an effort, when you examine the clock. But another stream of ideas carries you away; which might plunge you in an instant into a living whirlwind, and this other minute must be another eternity. For the proportions of time and of being are completely deranged by the multitude and the intensity of sensations and of ideas. One might say that one lives several lives in the space of an hour. Are you not then like a fantastic novel which ought to be living rather than written? There is no more equation between the other organs and one's enjoyments; and it is especially from this consideration that the disapproval applicable to this dangerous exercise where liberty disappears, surges.

When I speak of hallucinations you must not take the word in its strictest sense. A very subtle shade distinguishes the pure hallucination, such as doctors have often had occasion of studying, from the hallucination or rather from the scorn of the senses in the mental state caused by Haschisch. In the first case, the hallucination is sudden, perfect and fatal; besides, it finds no pretext nor excuse in the world of exterior objects. The intoxicated man sees a form, hears sounds where there are none. In the second case, the hallucination is progressive, almost voluntary, and it does not become perfect, it only attains ripeness by the action of the imagination. Finally, it has a pretext. Sound will speak, will say distinct things, but it will have a sound. The drunken eyes of the man who has taken Haschisch will see strange forms; but, before being strange or monstrous, these forms were simple and natural. Energy, the veritably speaking vivacity of the hallucination in intoxication, deforms in no sense this original difference. This has taken root in the surrounding soil, and in the present time, that has no root.

To make one understand better this overflow of imagination, this mixture of dreams and hallucinations to which is condemned a brain intoxicated by

Haschisch, I shall give this confession. It is a woman, rather a mature woman, curious, of an excitable spirit, who, having yielded to the temptation of using the drug, describes her visions. This I transcribe literally.

"However bizarre and astonishing are these sensations that intoxicate my folly for twelve hours (twelve or twenty?—I don't know which), I shall never return to them. The spiritual excitement is too vivid, the fatigue too much to endure, and, to say all, in this childish enchantment I find something criminal. Finally, I yielded to the curiosity; and this was a folly in common, in the house of two old friends, where I saw no harm in losing some of my dignity. Before all, I ought to say to you that the accursed Haschisch is certainly a perfidious substance: one sometimes imagines one can get rid of the intoxication, but this is no more than a deceptive calm. There are reposes in it, and then respites. Thus, at ten o'clock at night, I found myself in one of these momentary states; I imagined I was delivered from this superabundance of life which had caused me such intense pleasure, but which was not without fear and disquietude. I began by enjoying my dinner, yet as if I were harassed by a long voyage. For up to this moment, by prudence, I had abstained from eating. But, before I rose from the table my delirium returned to me as a cat seizes a mouse, and the poison began again to play evil tricks with my poor brain. Although my house was at some distance from my friends' chateau, and though there was a carriage waiting for me, I felt so utterly invaded with the desire of dreaming and of abandoning myself to this irresistible folly, that I joyfully accepted their invitation for me to remain there till the next day. You knew the chateau; you knew that they had arranged and *modernised* the modern part in which they lived—those it belongs to—but that the part which is generally unused has been left as it was, with its old style and its old decorations. They decided to improvise for me a bedroom in this part of the chateau, and they chose for me the smallest of all these rooms, a kind of boudoir rather decrepit and faded, but none the less charming. I must describe it to you as far as I can—*tant bien que mal*—so that you can understand the singular vision of which I was the victim; a vision which never left me for one entire night, during which I had no chance of perceiving the flight of the hours.

"This boudoir was very small, very narrow. At the height of the cornice the ceiling has the aspect of a vault; the walls are covered with long mirrors, separated by panels on which are painted landscapes in the awkward style of decoration. At the height of the cornice, on the four walls, allegorical figures are represented, some in reposeful attitudes, the others running and flying. Above them are painted some brilliant birds and flowers. Behind the figures I saw a deceptive trellis which follows naturally the curve of the ceiling, which is gilded. All the interstices between the magic wands and the figures are gilded, and in the centre the gilt is only interrupted by the geometrical network. You see that's rather like a very distinguished cage, a very lovely cage for a very big bird. I must add that the night was wonderful, transparent, the moon a half-crescent, but so vivid that, even after I extinguished the candle, the whole decoration was visible, not illuminated by my own vision, as you ought to believe, but lightened by this adorable night, whose reflections fell on these pale gold ornaments, mirrors and fantastic mixtures of colours.

"I was at first astonished to see great spaces extend themselves before me, on both sides; there were limpid lakes and green verdure and tranquil waters. You can divine what I mean by the panels being reverberated by the mirrors. As I lifted my eyes I saw a sunset like metal in fusion, as it became frigid. This was the gilt of the ceiling; but the trellis made me think I was confined in a kind of cage or in a house open on all sides on vacant space, and that I was only separated from all these marvels by the bars of my magnificent prison. I began to laugh at my illusion; but the more I regarded it, the more magical it became, the more life it assumed, the more despotic became the reality. From that instant the idea of confinement dominated my spirit, without too much disturbing, I ought to say, the varied sensations given me by the spectacle around and above me. I imagined that I was imprisoned for a great length of time, perhaps for millions of years, in this sumptuous cage, in the midst of fairy-like landscapes, between miraculous horizons. I dreamed of *la Belle aux bois dormant,* of an expiation I had to endure, of a future deliverance. Over my head fluttered brilliant tropical birds, and as my ear perceived the sound of little bells on the necks of the horses who went their way on the high road, both sounds fusing their impressions in one unique idea, I attributed to the birds the mysterious song of bronze, and I believed that they sang with metal throats. Evidently they were talking about me as they celebrated my captivity. Mocking monkeys and comic satyrs seemed to amuse themselves immensely with this extended prisoner—the woman who writes to you!—condemned to an utter immobility. But all the mythological deities gazed on me with sardonic smiles, as if to encourage me to endure patiently the witchcraft, and their malicious pupils glided into the corners of their eyelids as if to attach themselves to my regard. I concluded that if ancient faults, if certain sins unknown to me, had needed this temporary chastisement, I could count all the same on some superior power, which, while it condemned me, might offer me pleasures ever so much graver than those of the dolls who enchant our youth. You saw that these moral considerations were not absent from my dream; but I ought to avow that the pleasure I had in contemplating these brilliant colours and forms, and of believing myself the centre of a fantastic drama, frequently absorbed all my other thoughts. This state endured a long, long time —I can't conceive how long I endured it. Did I endure it till dawn? That I ignore. I saw suddenly the sun illuminate my room; I experienced a vivid astonishment, and despite all the efforts in the way of memory I could make, it was impossible to me to know if I had slept or if I had patiently submitted to a delicious insomnia. To begin with, it was the night, and, to end with, it was the day! And yet I had lived, lived, lived—I know not how many myriads of existences! The notion of time or rather the measure of time was abolished, the entire night was memorable for me only by the multitude of my thoughts. Enormous, as this length of time appeared to me from my point of view, it always seemed to me that it had not endured more than several seconds, or even that it had not taken place in eternity.

"I don't speak to you of my fatigue—it was immense. I have heard that the enthusiasm of poets and of creators is not unlike what I have experienced, in spite of the fact that I have always imagined that such men whose delight is to move us ought to be of a really calm temperament; but if poetical delirium has any resemblance with what a little teaspoonful of drugged jam has given me, I think that all such pleasures cost dear to poets, and it is not without a certain prosaic satisfaction that I return to real life, *que je me suis enfin chez moi, dans mon chez moi intellectuel*."

This is evidently a reasonable woman; I shall only make use of her confessions by way of adding to them certain notes which ought to conclude this very summary description of the principal sensations caused by Haschisch.

She spoke of the dinner as of a fortunate pleasure, at the moment when a momentary embellishment of things, which seemed definite, permitted her to return to real life. In effect there are, as I have said, deceptive calms and intermittences, and often Haschisch determines a voracious hunger, almost always an excessive thirst. Only the dinner or the supper, instead of causing a definite relief, created this unexpected exasperation, this vertiginous crisis of which this woman complained, and which was followed by a series of enchanting visions, somewhat touched by fear, to which she had positively resigned herself. This tyrannical thirst and hunger of which there is question are not satiated without an immensity of labour. For man believes himself lifted to such a height above material things, or rather he is so overwhelmed by his intoxication, that he has to show a certain amount of courage so as to shake a bottle.

The definite crisis determined by the digestion of one's food is in effect very violent; it is impossible to fight against it; and such a state would be insupportable if it endured for too great a space of time, and if it did not soon give place to another phase of intoxication, which, in the aforesaid case, is translated by splendid visions, sweetly terrifying and full of consolations. This state is what the orientals name *Kief.* This is no more than something whirling and tumultuous, no more than an immobile isolation, no more than a glorious resignation. For a certain length of time you have not been master of yourself, but this causes an obsession, an exasperation. Sorrow and the sense of time having disappeared, or if anything else were to produce itself, it would be transfigured by the dominating sensation; and only relatively in its habitual form with what poetical melancholy is to positive sorrow.

But, above all, observe that in this woman's story (which I have transcribed) the hallucination is of a bastard kind, whose reason of being is that of an exterior spectacle; the mind is no more than a mirror where the surrounding environment is transformed in an extraordinary fashion. Besides, we see intervene what I must call the moral hallucination: the subject believes he is subjected to an expiation. The benevolent regard of the Olympian Deities is poetised by a kind of varnish essentially *Haschischin*. I cannot say that this woman has escaped from the sense of remorse; but that her thoughts, momentarily turned in the direction of melancholy and regret, have returned to their former sensibility. This is a remark I shall have occasion to verify.

She spoke of the fatigue of yesterday; in effect, this fatigue is always excessive, but it does not always manifest itself immediately, and, when you are obliged to recognise it, it is not without astonishment. For at first, when you are certain that a new dawn has risen on the horizon of your existence, you experience something wonderful; you imagine you are in possession of a marvellous spirituality. But no sooner are you out of bed, than all that remains of the intoxication follows and hinders you, like the chain of your recent servitude. You can hardly walk and you fear at every instant that you might break yourself like any fragile thing. An intense lassitude (there are some who pretend it is not without a charm of its own) seizes your mind and extends itself across your faculties, as a mist over a landscape. You find yourself, for some hours, incapable of work, of action, and of energy. This is the punishment of the impious prodigality with which you have spent your nervous fluid. You have disseminated your personality to the four winds of the world, and, now, what intensity of pain do you not experience in concentrating it and in gathering it together!

8. ‖ WILLIAM BLAIR

An Opium-Eater in America

Esse quid hoc dicam, quod tam mihi dura videntur
  Strata, neque in lecto pallia nostra sedent?
Et vacuus somno noctem, quam longa, peregi;
  Lassaque versati corporis ossa dolent.

Ovid, *Amor*

Before I state the results of my experience as an opium-eater, it will perhaps not be uninteresting, and it certainly will conduce to the clearer understanding of such statement, if I give a slight and brief sketch of my habits and history previous to my first indulgence in the infernal drug which has embittered my existence for seven most weary years.

The death of my father when I was little more than twelve months old made it necessary that I should receive only such an education as would qualify me to pursue some business in my native town of Birmingham; and in all probability I should at this moment be entering orders or making out invoices in that great emporium of buttons and blackguards, had I not (whether fortunately or otherwise I pretend not to decide) at a very early age evinced a decided and absorbing passion for reading, which the free access to a tolerably large library enabled me to indulge, until it had grown to be a confirmed habit of mind, which, when the attention of my *friends* was called to the subject, had become too strong to be broken through; and with the usual foolish family vanity they determined to indulge a taste so early and decidedly developed, in the expectation, I verily believe, of some day catching a reflected beam from the fame and glory which I was to win by my genius; for by that mystical name was the mere musty talent of a *helluo librorum* called. The consequence was that I was sent, when eight years of age, to a public school. I had however before this tormented my elder brother with ceaseless importunity, until he had consented to teach me Latin; and by secretly poring over my sister's books, I had contrived to gain a tolerable book-knowledge of French.

From that hour my fate was decided. I applied with unwearied devotion to the study of the classics —the only branch of education attended to in the school; and I even considered it a favor to be allowed to translate, write exercises and themes, and to compose Latin verses for the more idle of my school-fellows. At the same time I devoured all books of whatever description, which came in my way: poems, novels, history, metaphysics, or works of science, with an indiscriminating appetite, which has proved very injurious to me through life. I drank as eagerly of the muddy and stagnant pool of [dirty] literature, as of the pure and sparkling fountains glowing in the many-hued sun-light of genius. After two years had been spent in this manner, I was removed to another school, the principal of which, although a fair mathematician, was a wretched classical scholar. In fact I frequently construed passages of Virgil, which I had not previously looked at, when he himself was forced to refer to Davidson for assistance. I stayed with him, however, two years, during which time I spent all the money I could get in purchasing Greek and Hebrew books, of which languages I learned the rudiments, and obtained considerable knowledge without any instruction. After a year's residence at the house of my brother-in-law, which I passed in studying Italian and Persian, the Bishop of Litchfield's examining chaplain, to whom I had been introduced in terms of the most hyperbolical praise, prevailed on his diocesan and the Earl of Calthorpe to share the expense of my further education.

In consequence of this unexpected good fortune, I was now placed under the care of the Rev. Thomas Fry, Rector of the Village of Emberton in Buckinghamshire, a clergyman of great piety and profound learning, with whom I remained about fifteen months, pursuing the study of languages with increased ardor. During the whole of that period I never allowed myself more than four hours' sleep; and still unsatisfied, I very generally spent the whole night, twice a week, in the insane pursuit of those avenues of distinction to which alone my ambition was confined. I took no exercise, and the income allowed me was so small that I could not afford a meat dinner more than once a week, and at the same time set apart the half of that allowance for the purchase of books, which I had determined to do. I smoked incessantly; for I now required some stimulus, as my health was much injured by my unrelaxing industry. My digestion was greatly impaired; and the constitution of iron which Nature had given me threatened to break down ere long under the effects of the systematic neglect with which I treated its repeated warnings. I suffered from constant headache; my total inactivity caused the digestive organs to become torpid; and the innutritious nature of the food which I allowed myself would not supply me with the strength which my assiduous labor required. My nerves were dreadfully shaken; and at the age of fourteen I exhibited the external symptoms of old age. I was feeble and emaciated; and had this mode of life continued twelve months longer, I must have sank under it.

I had during those fifteen months thought and read much on the subject of revealed religion, and had devoted a considerable portion of my time to an examination of the evidences advanced by the advocates of Christianity, which resulted in a reluctant conviction of their utter weakness and inability. No sooner was I aware that so complete a change of opinion had taken place, then I wrote to my patron stating the fact, and explaining the process by which I had arrived at such a conclusion. The reply I received was a peremptory order to return to my mother's house immediately; and on arriving there, the first time I had entered it for some years, I was met by the information that I had nothing more to expect from the countenance of those who had supplied me with the means of prosecuting my studies to "so bad a purpose." I was so irritated by what I considered the unjustifiable harshness of this decision, that at the moment I wrote a haughty and angry letter to one of the parties, which of course widened the breach, and made the separation between us eternal.

What was I now to do? I was unfit for any business, by habit, inclination, and constitution. My health was ruined, and hopeless poverty stared me in the face; when a distinguished solicitor in my native town, who by the way has since become celebrated in the political world, offered to receive me as a clerk. I at once accepted the offer; but knowing that in my *then* condition it was impossible for me to perform the duties required of me, I decided on *taking opium!* The strange confessions of De Quincey had long been a favorite with me. The first part had in fact been given me both as a model in English composition, and also as an exercise to be rendered into Patavinian Latin. The latter part, the "Miseries of Opium," I had most unaccountably always neglected to read. Again and again, when my increasing debility had threatened to bring my studies to an abrupt conclusion, I had meditated this experiment, but an undefinable and shadowy fear had as often stayed my hand. But now that I knew that unless I could by artificial stimuli obtain a sudden increase of strength I must *starve* I no longer hesitated. I was desperate. I believed that something horrible would result from it, though my imagination, the most vivid, could not conjure up visions of horror half so terrific as the fearful reality. I knew that for every hour of comparative ease and comfort its treacherous alliance might confer upon me *now,* I must endure days of bodily suffering; but I did not, could not, conceive the mental hell into whose fierce corroding fires I was about to plunge!

All that occurred during the first day is imperishably engraved upon my memory. It was about a week previous to the day appointed for my début in my new character as an attorney's clerk; and when I arose, I was depressed in mind, and a racking pain, to which I had lately been subject, was maddening me. I could scarcely manage to crawl into the breakfast-room. I had previously procured a drachm of opium, and I took two grains with my coffee. It did not produce any change in my feelings. I took two more—still without effect; and by six o'clock in the evening I had taken ten grains. While I was sitting at tea, I felt a strange sensation, totally unlike any thing I had ever felt before; a gradual *creeping thrill,* which in a few minutes occupied every part of my body, lulling to sleep the before-mentioned racking pain, producing a pleasing glow from head to foot, and inducing a sensation of dreamy exhilaration (if the phrase be intelligible to others as it is to me), similar in nature but not in degree to the drowsiness caused by wine, though not inclining me to sleep; in fact so far from it, that I longed to engage in some active exercise; to sing, dance, or leap. I then resolved to go to the theatre—the last place I should the day before have dreamed of visiting; for the sight of cheerfulness in others made me doubly gloomy.

I went; and so vividly did I feel my vitality—for

in this state of delicious exhilaration even mere excitement seemed absolute elysium—that I could not resist the temptation to break out in the strangest vagaries, until my companions thought me deranged. As I ran up the stairs I rushed after and flung back every one who was above me. I escaped numberless beatings solely through the interference of my friends. After I had been seated a few minutes, the nature of the excitement was changed, and a "waking sleep" succeeded. The actors on the stage vanished; the stage itself lost its reality; and before my entranced sight magnificent halls stretched out in endless succession, with gallery above gallery, while the roof was blazing with gems, like stars whose rays alone illumined the whole building, which was thronged with strange, gigantic figures, like the wild possessors of a lost globe, such as Lord Byron has described in "Cain;" as beheld by the Fratricide, when guided by Lucifer he wandered among the shadowy existences of those worlds which had been destroyed to make way for our pigmy earth. I will not attempt further to describe the magnificent vision which a little pill of "brown gum" had conjured up from the realm of ideal being. No words that *I* can command would do justice to its Titanian splendor and immensity.

At midnight I was roused from my dreamy abstraction; and on my return home the blood in my veins seemed to "run lightning," and I knocked down (for I had the strength of a giant at that moment) the first watchman I met: of course there was "a row," and for some minutes a battle-royal raged in New Street, the principal thoroughfare of the town, between my party and the "Charleys"; who, although greatly superior in numbers, were sadly "milled"; for we were all somewhat scientific bruisters, that sublime art or science having been cultivated with great assiduity at the public school, through which I had as was customary fought my way. I reached home at two in the morning with a pair of "Oxford spectacles" which confined me to the house for a week. I slept disturbedly, haunted by terrific dreams and oppressed by the Night-mare and her nine-fold, and awoke with a dreadful headache; stiff in every joint, and with deadly sickness of the stomach, which lasted for two or three days; my throat contracted and parched, my tongue furred, my eyes bloodshot, and the whole surface of my body burning hot. I did not have recourse to opium again for three days; for the strength it had excited did not till then fail me. When partially recovered from the nausea the first dose had caused, my spirits were good, though not exuberant; but I could eat nothing, and was annoyed by an insatiable thirst. I went to the office, and for six months performed the services required of me without lassitude or depression of spirits; though never again did I experience the same delicious sensations as on that memorable night, which is an "oasis in the desert" of my subsequent existence; life I cannot call it, for the *vivida vis animi et corporis* was extinct.

In the seventh month my misery commenced. Burning heat, attended with constant thirst, then began to torment me from morning till night: my skin became scurfy; the skin of my feet and hands peeled off; my tongue was always furred; a feeling of contraction in the bowels was continual; my eyes were strained and discolored, and I had unceasing head-ache. But internal and external heat was the pervading feeling and appearance. My digestion became still weaker, and my incessant costiveness was painful in the extreme. The reader must not however imagine that all these symptoms appeared suddenly and at once; they came on gradually, though with frightful rapidity, until I became a *morborum moles,* as a Romanic physician whose lucubrations I met with and perused with great amusement some years since in a little country alehouse (God knows how it got there) poetically expresses it. I could not sleep for hours after I had lain down, and consequently was unable to rise in time to attend the office in the morning, though as yet no visions of horror haunted my slumbers. Mr. P, my employer, bore with this for some months; but at length his patience was wearied; and I was informed that I must attend at nine in the morning. I could not; for even if I rose at seven, after two or three hours' unhealthy and fitful sleep, I was unable to walk or exert myself in any way for at least two hours. I was at this time taking laudanum, and had no appetite for any thing but coffee and acid fruits. I could and did drink great quantities of ale, though it would not, as nothing would, quench my thirst.

Matters continued in this state for fifteen months, during which time the only comfortable hours I spent were in the evening, when freed from the du-

ties of the office, I sat down to study, which it is
rather singular I was able to do with as strong zest
and as unwearied application as ever; as will appear,
when I mention that in those fifteen months I read
through in the evenings the whole of Cicero, Tacitus,
the Corpus Poetarum (Latinorum), Boëthius, Scip-
tores Historiæ Augustinæ, Homer, Corpus Græ-
carum Tragediarum, a great part of Plato, and a
large mass of philological works. In fact, in the evening I generally felt comparatively well, not being
troubled with many of the above mentioned symptoms. These evenings were the very happiest of my
life. I had ample means for the purchase of books,
for I lived very cheap on bread, ale, and coffee; and
I had access to a library containing all the Latin classics—Valpy's edition in one hundred and fifty volumes, octavo, a magnificent publication—and about
fifteen thousand other books. Toward the end of the
year 1829 I established at my own expense and
edited myself a magazine by which I lost a considerable sum; though the pleasure I derived from
my monthly labors amply compensated me. In
December of that year my previous sufferings became light in comparison with those which now
seized upon me, never completely to leave me again.

One night, after taking about fifty grains of
opium, I sat down in my arm-chair to read the confession of a Russian who had murdered his brother
because he was the chosen of her whom both loved.
It was recorded by a French priest who visited him
in his last moments, and was powerfully and elo-
quently written. I dozed while reading it; and imme-

diately I was present in the prison-cell of the Fratricide; I saw his ghastly and death-dewed features, his
despairing yet defying look, the gloomy and impenetrable dungeon; the dying lamp, which seemed but to
render "Darkness visible"; and the horror-struck yet
pitying expression of the priest's countenance; *but
there I lost my identity*. Though *I* was the recipient
of these impressions, yet I was not myself separately
and distinctively existent and sentient; but my entity
was confounded with that of not only the two figures
before me, but of the inanimate objects surrounding
them. This state of compound existence I can no farther describe. While in this state I composed the
"Fratricide's Death," [a poem], or rather it composed *itself* and forced itself upon my memory
without any activity or volition on my part.

And here again another phenomenon presented itself. The images reflected, if the expression be al-
lowable, in the verses rose bodily and with perfect
distinctness before me, simultaneously with their verbal representatives; and when I roused myself (I had
not been *sleeping* but was only *abstracted*) all remained clear and distinct in my memory. From that
night for six months darkness always brought the
most horrible fancies and opticular and auricular or
acoustical delusions of a frightful nature, so vivid
and real, that instead of a blessing, sleep became a
curse; and the hours of darkness became hours
which seemed days of misery. For many consecutive
nights I dared not undress myself nor "put out the
light," lest the moment I lay down some *monstrum
horrendum, informe, ingens* should blast my sight

with his hellish aspect! I had a double sense of sight and sound; one real, the other visonary; both equally strong and apparently real; so that while I distinctly heard imaginary footsteps ascending the stairs, the door opening, and my curtains drawn, I at the same time as plainly heard any actual sound in or outside the house, and could not remark the slightest difference between them; and while I *saw* an imaginary assassin standing by my bed bending over me with a lamp in one hand and a dagger in the other, I could see any real tangible object which the degree of light that might be then in the room made visible. Though these visionary rears and imaginary objects had presented themselves to me every night for months, yet I never could convince myself of their non-existence; and every fresh appearance caused suffering of as intense and as deadly horror as on the first night! And so great was the confusion of the real with the unreal, that I nearly became a convert to Bishop Berkeley's non-reality doctrines. My health was also rapidly becoming worse; and before I had taken my opium in the morning, I had become unable to move hand or foot, and of course could not rise from my bed until I had received strength from the "damnable dirt." I could not attend the office at all in the morning, and was forced to throw up my articles, and as the only chance left me of gaining a livelihood, turn to writing for magazines for support. I left B. and proceeded to London, where I engaged with Charles Knight to supply the chapters on the use of elephants in the wars of the ancients for the "History of Elephants," then preparing for publication in the series of the Library of Entertaining Knowledge. For this purpose I obtained permission to use the Library of the British Museum for six months, and again devoted myself with renewed ardor to my favorite studies.

But "what a falling off was there!" My memory was impaired; and in reading I was conscious of a confusion of mind which prevented my clearly comprehending the full meaning of what I read. Some organ appeared to be defective. My judgment too was weakened, and I was frequently guilty of the most absurd actions, which at the time I considered wise and prudent. The strong common sense which I had at one time boasted of, deserted me. I lived in a dreamy, imaginative state, which completely disqualified me for managing my own affairs. I spent large sums of money in a day, and then starved for a month; and all this while the *châteaux en Espagne,* which had once only afforded me an idle amusement, now usurped the place of the realities of life, and led me into many errors, and even unjustifiable acts of immorality, which lowered me in the estimation of my acquaintances and friends, who saw the effect but never dreamed the cause. Even those who knew I was an opium-eater, not being aware of the effects which the habitual use of it produced, attributed my mad conduct to either want of principle or aberration of intellect; and I thus lost several of my best friends, and temporarily alienated many others.

After a month or two passed in this employment, I regained a portion of strength sufficient to enable me to obtain a livelihood by reporting on my own account in the courts of law in Westminister any cause which I judged of importance enough to afford a reasonable chance of selling again; and by supplying reviews and occasional original articles to the periodicals, the Monthly, the New Monthly, Metropolitan, etc. My health continued to improve, probably in consequence of my indulging in higher living and taking much more exercise than I had done for two or three years; as I had no need of buying books, having the use of at least five hundred thousand volumes in the Museum. I was at last fortunate enough to obtain the office of parliamentary reporter to a morning paper, which produced about three hundred pounds a year; but after working on an average fourteen or fifteen hours a day for a few months, I was obliged to resign the situation, and again depend for support on the irregular employment I had before been engaged in, and for which I was now alone fit. My constitution now appeared to have completely sunk under the destroying influence of the immense quantity of opium I had for some months taken—two hundred, two hundred and fifty, and three hundred grains a day. I was frequently obliged to repeat the dose several times a day, as my stomach had become so weak that the opium would not remain upon it; and I was besides afflicted with continual vomiting after having eaten any thing. I really believed that I could not last much longer. Tic-douloureux was also added to my other sufferings; constant headache, occasional spasms, heart-burn, pains in the legs and back, and a general irritability of the nerves, which would not allow me to remain above a few minutes in the same position. My temper became soured and morose. I was careless of every thing, and drank to excess, in the hope of thus supplying the place of the stimulus which had lost its power.

At length I was compelled to keep to my bed by a violent attack of pleurisy, which has since seized me about the same time every year. My digestion was so thoroughly ruined, that I was frequently almost maddened by the suffering which indigestion occasioned. I could not sleep, though I was no longer troubled with visions, which had left me about three months. At last I became so ill that I was forced to leave London and visit my mother in Kenilworth, where I stayed; writing occasionally, and instructing a few pupils in Greek and Hebrew. I was also now compelled to sell my library, which contained several Arabic and Persian *manuscripts,* a complete collection of Latin authors, and nearly a complete one of Greek; a large collection of Hebrew and Rabbinic works, which I had obtained at a great expense and with great trouble—all went; the only relics of it I was able to retain were the "Corpus Poetarum, Græcorum et Latinorum"; and I have never since been able to collect another library. Idleness, good living, and constant exercise, revived me; but with returning strength my nocturnal visitors returned, and again my nights were made dreadful. I was "terrified through visions" similar to those which had so alarmed me at first, and I was obliged to drink deeply at night to enable me to sleep at all.

In this state I continued till June, 1833, when I

determined once more to return to London; and I left Kenilworth without informing any one of my intention the night before. The curate of the parish called at my lodgings to inform me that he had obtained the gift of six hundred pounds to enable me to reside at Oxford until I could graduate. Had I stayed twenty-four hours longer, I should not now be living in hopeless poverty in a foreign country; but pursuing under more favorable auspices than ever brightened my path before those studies which supported and cheered me in poverty and illness, and with a fair prospect of obtaining that learned fame for which I had longed so ardently from my boyhood, and in the vain endeavor to obtain which I had sacrificed my health and denied myself not only the pleasures and luxuries but even the necessaries of life. I had while at the office in B. entered my name on the books of Brazen-nose College, Oxford, and resided there one term, not being able to afford the expense attendant on a longer residence. Thus it has been with me through life. Fortune has again and again thrown the means of success in my way, but they have been like the waters of Tantalus, alluring but to escape from my grasp the moment I approached to seize them.

I remained in London only a few days, and then proceeded to Amsterdam, where I stayed a week, and then went to Paris. After completely exhausting my stock of money, I was compelled to walk back to Calais, which I did with little inconvenience, as I found that money was unneccessary; the only difficulty I met with being how to escape from the overflowing hospitality I everywhere experienced from rich and poor. My health was much improved when I arrived in town, and I immediately proceeded on foot to Birmingham, where I engaged with Doctor Palmer, a celebrated physician, to supply the Greek and Latin synonymes, and correct the press for a dictionary of the terms used by the French in medicine, which he was preparing. The pay I received was so very small that I was again reduced to the poorest and most meagre diet; and an attack of pleurisy produced such a state of debility that I was compelled to leave Birmingham and return to my mother's house in Kenilworth.

I had now firmly resolved to free myself from my fatal habit; and the very day I reached home I began to diminish the quantity I was then taking by one grain per day. I received the most careful attention, and every thing was done that could add to my comfort and alleviate the sufferings I must inevitably undergo. Until I had arrived at seventeen and a half grains a day I experienced but little uneasiness, and my digestive organs acquired or regained strength very rapidly. All constipation had vanished. My skin became moist and more healthy, and my spirits instead of being depressed became equable and cheerful. No visions haunted my sleep. I could not sleep, however, more than two or three hours at a time; and from about three a.m. until eight, when I took my opium, I was restless, and troubled with a gnawing, twitching sensation in the stomach. From seventeen grains downward my torment (for by that word alone can I characterize the pangs I endured) com-

menced. I could not rest, either lying, sitting, or
standing. I was compelled to change my position
every moment; and the only thing that relieved me
was walking about the country. My sight became
weak and dim; the gnawing at my stomach was perpetual, resembling the sensation caused by ravenous
hunger; but food, though I ate voraciously, would
not relieve me. I also felt a sinking in the stomach,
and such a pain in the back that I could not
straighten myself up. A dull constant aching pain
took possession of the calves of my legs; and there
was a continual jerking motion of the nerves from
head to foot. My head ached; my intellect was terri-
bly weakened and confused. I could not think, talk,
read or write; to sleep was impossible, until by walking from morning till night I had so thoroughly tired
myself that pain could not keep me awake; although
I was so weak that walking was misery to me. And
yet under all these désagréments I did not feel de-
jected in spirits; although I became unable to walk,
and used to lie on the floor and roll about in agony
for hours together. I should certainly have taken
opium again, if the chemist had not, by my mother's
instruction, refused to sell it. I became worse every
day; and it was not till I had entirely left off the
drug, two months nearly, that any alleviation of my
suffering was perceptible. I gradually but very slowly
recovered my strength, both of mind and body;
though it was long before I could read or write, or
even converse. My appetite was too good; for though
while an opium-eater I could not endure to taste the
smallest morsel of fat, I now could eat at dinner a

pound of bacon which had not a hair's breadth of lean in it.

The fifteenth of May was the first day I was entirely free from pain. Previous to my arrival in Kenilworth, an intimate friend of mine had been ruined—reduced at once from affluence to utter penury by the villainy of his partner, to whom he had entrusted the whole of his business, and who had committed two forgeries, for which he was sentenced to transportation for life. In consequence of this event, my friend, who was a little older than myself, and had been about twelve months married, determined to leave his young wife and child, and seek to rebuild his broken fortunes in Canada. When he informed me that such was his plan, I resolved to accompany him, and immediately commenced the necessary preparations for my voyage. I was not however ready, not having been able so soon to collect the sum necessary, when he was obliged to leave; and as I could not have him for my *compagnon du voyage,* I altered my course and took my passage for New York, in the vain hope and expectation of obtaining a better income here, where the ground was comparatively unoccupied, than in London, where there were hundreds of men as well qualified as myself dependent on literature for their support.

I need not add how lamentably I was disappointed. The first inquiries I made [after arriving in New York] were met by advice to endeavor to obtain a livelihood by some other profession than authorship. I could get no employment as a reporter; and the applications I addressed to the editors of several of the daily newspapers received no answer. My prospects appeared as gloomy as they could well be, and my spirits sunk beneath the pressure of the anxious cares which now weighed so heavily upon me. I was alone in a strange country, without an acquaintance into whose ear I might pour the gathering bitterness of my blighted hopes. I was also much distressed by the intense heat of July, which kept me from morning till night in a state much like that occasioned by a vapor-bath. I was so melancholy and hopeless that I really found it necessary to have recourse to either brandy or opium. I preferred the latter, although to ascertain the difference, merely as a philosophical experiment, I took rather copious draughts of the former also. But observe; I did not intend ever again to become the slave of opium. I merely proposed to take three or four grains a day, until I should procure some literary engagement, and until the weather became more cool. All my efforts to obtain such engagements were in vain; and I should undoubtedly have sunk into hopeless despondency, had not a gentleman (to whom I had brought an order for a small sum of money, twice the amount of which he had insisted on my taking) perceiving how deeply and injuriously I was affected by my repeated disappointments, offered me two hundred dollars to write "Passages from the life of an Opium-Eater," in two volumes. I gladly accepted this generous and disinterested offer; but before I had written more than two or three sheets, I became disgusted with the subject. I attempted to proceed, but found that my former facility in composition had deserted me; that in fact I could not write. I now discovered that the attempt to leave off opium again would be one of doubtful result. I had increased my quantum to forty grains. I again became careless and inert; and I believe that the short time that had elapsed since I had broken the habit in England had not been sufficient to allow my system to free itself from the poison which had been so long undermining its powers. I could not at once leave it off; and in truth I was not very anxious to do so, as it enabled me to forget the difficulties of the situation in which I had placed myself; while I knew that with regained freedom the cares and troubles which had caused me again to flee to my destroyer for relief would press upon my mind with redoubled weight. I remained in Brooklyn until November. Since then I have resided in the city, in great poverty; frequently unable to procure a dinner; as the few dollars I received from time to time scarcely sufficed to supply me with opium. Whether I shall now be able to leave off opium, God only knows! But whether I do or not, I have no hope whatever of gaining a respectable livelihood in this country; and I shall therefore return to England the moment I can obtain a passage.

Section IV | The Way Out

9. CHAMAN NAHAL

J. Krishnamurti on Self

October 20, 1964. Place: J. Krishnamurti's room in the home of his hostess, in New Delhi.

The room is austere. There is a bed in one corner, a table and a chair in another, two or three more chairs. A door opens on the verandah, and in the distance I can see the gardener mowing the lawn.

I am meeting J. Krishnamurti for the second time in five years. The first time was in 1959, when after listening to one of his talks I had gone and spent a few minutes with him. He comes in, not much changed since 1959, looking neat and handsome, erect in his bearing in spite of his age, his grey hair properly groomed, and his face sincere and open, his eyes big and penetrating. He folds his hands in greeting.

Krishnamurti: Please sit down.

I sit on the bed. He draws a chair near to me. I explain that since 1959 I had never felt the need to come and personally see him. That his message, or whatever he wanted to communicate, was so simple and direct that it had made its impact on me and I

*did not think I needed a further explanation from
him.*

Krishnamurti (*interrupting*): What has happened
now, sir?

Nahal: Well——. (*I fumble and stop, unable to
think of a suitable reply.*)

Nahal: It is very peaceful here, sir!

*Krishnamurti says nothing to this. He smiles,
leans forward and gently touches me on the knee, as
if to tell me to relax. He does not repeat his enquiry
about the purpose of my visit.*

Nahal (*stressing the words*): But it *is* very peaceful. It was like this when I met you on the former occasion—equally peaceful. Many other visitors to you
have also spoken of it, the calm and harmony that
suddenly descends. . . . (*Giving a definite shape to
my thoughts*) Is there any element of hypnosis in it,
sir?

Nahal (*continuing after a brief pause*): You
know persons like Gurdjieff and Mme. Blavatsky
were accused of hypnotising their listeners, paralys-
ing them, so to say, and inducing in them a state of
well-being. I should like to know if the peace that I
am experiencing this moment is by any chance on
account of some controlled effort on your part. Or is
it there independent of both of us?

Krishnamurti: I assure you, sir, I do not practice
hypnotism nor have any faith in it.

Nahal: What is this tranquillity then that I am experiencing? From where has it arrived? How?

Krishnamurti: Is your experiencing of this particular feeling you refer to dependent on first finding out an answer to its origin?

Nahal: No, I don't think so. Still I should like to know. I am interested in discovering the causes which affect and change our consciousness. Are you aware of the experiments to alter human consciousness with the use of drugs?

Krishnamurti: You mean mescalin and that kind of stuff?

Nahal: Yes. (*And then, remembering something*) Your friend, Aldous Huxley, also experimented with it.

Krishnamurti (*waving his hand, impatiently*): Well, Aldous used to discuss it with me, but of course the whole thing is meaningless. Why go so far? We all know that human consciousness can be disturbed with stimulants. An alcoholic drink will do that much for you. But then you are back next morning where you were before, when the effect of the drink is gone, feeling worse and miserable for your experience. Truly great experiences are those which happen on their own, sir, without any effort on the part of the individual to manipulate them—for himself or for others.

Nahal: Would you apply this to experiences gained through Yoga? What of the yogis who claim to go into trances, or who practice developing into a super-conscious state of mind?

Krishnamurti: The same, sir. These experiences, however profound they may appear to be, remain within the sphere of time. For me hypnosis, drugs or yoga are all attempts at self-delusion.

Nahal: Some time back I saw a book by you in a British library, where you speak of leading others to light, provided they followed you. It was published in 1926.

Krishnamurti (*with a reminiscent smile*): Ah, yes. That was when I was associated with The Order of the Star in the East. But I've moved away from that position. I don't offer to lead anyone now.

Nahal (*not sure if he would be willing to discuss such a personal matter any further*): Why did you break with that Order, sir? Was it a change of attitudes in you?—I'm sure Mrs. Annie Besant must have been heartbroken!

Krishnamurti: It was not a change of "attitudes." It was a total change which I exprienced, if I may put it that way. I felt that the truth about life had to be discovered by each individual for himself. The whole concept of Gurus and Followers became unreal to me, and I had to step aside from a position which I realised was a false one. (*He smiles, leans forward and holds my hand.*) No, sir, Mrs. Annie Besant was not heartbroken. (*Looking sad, and continuing to smile*) You know, sir, I was like a son to her. She actually agreed with my way of thinking. What worried her, and worried her a good deal, was the physical part of my life. The Order was a very rich organisation, and she didn't know how I would feed myself if I left it and went away.—But she sympathised with my outlook.

Nahal: But you have been teaching all the same, as a *guru*.

Krishnamurti: No, sir, no. I have been teaching, but at a totally different level. I am certainly all for sharing one's thoughts with others. In that light, I would be willing to accept any of the great teachers, Christ or Buddha or anyone else. I only object to a cult being woven around them, where the figure of the teacher becomes more important than his words or his thoughts.

Nahal: What exactly is your objection to established religions?

Krishnamurti: I think I've partly answered the question. Man's discovery of God ceases to be a discovery if he begins this search with a foregone conclusion in his mind. Most religions impose a certain image of the type of God they would want their followers to worship. Whereas to my mind, in the search for truth, which to me is the search for God, the choice does not rest with us as to what to reject or accept. Truth, God, call it what you will, is an awareness of the totality of existence, of our hopes and desires, our ambitions, our greed, our loves and thousands of other emotions which constitute what

passes for the living individual. I believe organised
religions stand in the way of this awareness of the totality of existence.

Nahal: In your teaching, you do not give the mind
a very big place. You say that it plays a dubious role
in our discovery of God. One must come to God,
you declare, without the conditioning imposed on us
by our knowledge and memories. Would you say
that animals, who do not have developed minds or
memories, are happier than human beings and closer
to reality?

Krishnamurti (*chuckles and answers at once*): Of
course not, sir. That's ridiculous. Mind has its own
place, a unique place in our lives. Without the use of
your mind you won't be able to find your way back
home, and I won't be able to conduct this conversation without its help. But mind can only move in the
sphere of the known, in the sphere of time. Whereas
we refer to God as the unknown, the timeless, is it
not? Till a certain stage in the three dimensional
world, our mind can serve us to our advantage. But
to reach the fourth dimension of existence, the mind,
instead of moving along the horizontal plan, must
learn to shoot up vertically as it were and explode
for the timeless, for the unknown to be.

Nahal: How do you see this worked out in practice, in the routine life of the millions who seek God?

Krishnamurti: In their sensitivity, sir, in their ability to remain open for the new. I do not like the
word God; it smacks of anthropomorphism. But in a

man's sensitivity to, in his choiceless awareness of, the totality of existence, in this alone, I find whatever meaning the word God conveys.

Nahal: What according to you is the most important problem of the day-to-day living?

Krishnamurti: You speak, sir, as if these were two different issues—that for so many hours a week we seek God and for so many attend to what you call the day-to-day living. To me, the two are identical. If anything, the day-to-day living is more valuable for me, for it is through this that one understands the meaning of existence.

Nahal: How do you see this day-to-day living properly carried out?

Krishnamurti (*rubbing his hands together*): In relationships which are moving and not static. That is the most vital issue, sir. We form a relationship and later get into the habit of looking at it from a fixed point of view—whether the relationship is with one's wife, or one's neighbours. Such relationships cease to be creative; they become dead. To have a moving relationship one has to be aware of the others as they are, from moment to moment, one has to be responsive to them, in short one has to be sensitive. Habit of any kind dulls sensitivity. We must be willing to accept the change in others and willing to change ourselves. "Willing" is perhaps not the correct expression. If we are sensitive, we cannot help noticing how time and circumstances modify others and we cannot help being impressed ourselves by the

same process. Sensitivity demands the ability to have
a serene mind, a mind which is not preoccupied with
itself, a mind which is receptive, which is an open
mind, a mind which is not always getting hurt at
what it sees or perceives.

Nahal: What about the spontaneous reaction if
someone is rude to you? You cannot help being hurt
at unprovoked hostility shown towards you, can
you?

Krishnamurti (*forcefully*): Well, I am not speaking of reaction. If someone sticks a pin into you, you
are bound to react—protect yourself, or cry out in
pain, or take yourself away from the offending agent
—your reaction depending on several factors, varying from man to man. I mean hurt in the sense of
nursing hatred. An event is over and for years we
keep brooding over it, working ourselves up into a
state of passion. The challenge of existence ever demands a fresh approach on our part to an issue or to
an individual. A mind which nurses hatred, or for
that matter nurses joy, long after the event is over,
ceases to be sensitive. Sensitivity is my equivalent of
meditation, which brings you its own rewards.

Nahal: How can one achieve this sensitivity?

Krishnamurti: By being what you really are. By
trying to see what *is*. You see, sir, genetically, or
through earlier conditioning, I have acquired a certain type of character. It is there, a part of myself,
like my nose or the shape of my chin. Now I must
try and see myself as I am, and I must make no

effort to be anything else. (*Finding me restless*) Just listen, sir. I am not advocating self-indulgence, that a hypocrite should continue to be a hypocrite or a thief remain a thief. I should not submit to my weakness, but I should not indulge in the opposite of my weakness either as a way of getting rid of it.

I am on the point of protesting, but J. Krishnamurti restrains me.

Krishnamurti: I'll make it clear, sir, just listen. Let us say I am given to hating others. Now I must not go and start loving them, making love as a panacea for my foolish temperament. That way I shall never learn to grow out of my hateful nature. I will only be generating contradictions in myself, running from one conflict to another. What is wanted of me is to accept the fact that I hate others and then go into the cause of this. I should ask myself: why do I hate? Is it that I expect too much from life? Am I in any respect frustrated? What is it that I want? Am I capable enough to get it? I should ask myself all this, and stay in this state of exploration, without making any deliberate effort on my part to get rid of my malady. Suddenly I will discover that a transformation takes place in myself, without any planning on my part, a creative transformation. My sensitivity has now come into play!

Nahal (*staggered at the enormity of what has just been outlined and seeing at once its meaning*): Will you say something on Death, sir, a fear which haunts most of us?

Krishnamurti (*smiles, leans forward and again takes my hand in his, and speaks with compassion*): It is a fear, sir, only if we see death as an event in time. We imagine death waiting for us far ahead and in the course of the years we build up a terror of this enemy which is lying behind the bush to pounce on us. Now, sir, the thing to do is to bring death closer to our daily life. Instead of letting it sit there at the other end of our life, let us bring it nearer, to the present day. We will discover then that death is there in everything, in our relationship with others, in the cells of our body as we continue to live, a constant change which is the law of life. If we keep this fact before us and learn the art of dying every day to some part of ourselves, to old memories, old relationships, the fear of death will vanish. The art of living to a large extent consists of learning the art of dying. It will then give rise to that play of sensitivity about which I spoke earlier. The actual death of the body one day, as you know, is unavoidable.

Nahal: But what do you think of the hereafter?

Krishnamurti: No one knows the answer, sir.

Nahal: But do you hold out the hope of some kind of survival of man's personality after death?

Krishnamurti: That is the repetitive desire of holding on to the known, to the familiar facets of life, is it not? The hereafter, sir, belongs to the unknown. Any attempt to affirm or deny its existence will take us away from the truth of it, which truth is that no one knows the answer.

Nahal: I have refrained from mentioning names and authorities in this conversation. But would you agree with those who find affinities in you and Buddhism or Zen or other schools of thought?

Krishnamurti: It is not for me to agree or disagree. But most of these schools, whether it is Buddhism, or Vedanta, or any other, suggest a "path"— the middle path, the negative path and the like. I suggest no path at all. For a path implies effort or practice, and the immeasurable can only be faced by a person by keeping himself free of effort, in a state of alert readiness for the new, in a state without fear or hope.

Nahal: You have consistently spoken against ideals, sir. How about the artists—the writers, the painters and the whole tribe of them—who are constantly building up utopias before us?

Krishnamurti: Artists are mischief-makers in this respect.

Nahal: In what respect, if any, are they an asset to society?

Krishnamurti: In being more sensitive, more alive to life than most of us are. An artist can make us aware of a whole range of new feelings. But (*with a look of pain on his face*) new feelings do not merely mean new forms of expression. Most modern art, or modern poetry and modern fiction, is bogged down with a craze for novelty of expression. An artist must first have a new awareness, a new something to say, and the form will of its own achieve a newness and freshness. But modern artists seem to be so impoverished and empty, inwardly. . . .

The meeting comes to an end here. J. Krishnamurti conducts me outside. He folds his hands, smiles at me, and with a bow disappears into his room.

10. RALPH WALDO EMERSON

The Over-Soul

The Supreme Critic on the errors of the past and the present, and the only prophet of that which must be, is that great nature in which we rest as the earth lies in the soft arms of the atmosphere; that Unity, that Over-soul, within which every man's particular being is contained and made one with all other; that common heart of which all sincere conversation is the worship, to which all right action is submission; that overpowering reality which confutes our tricks and talents, and constrains every one to pass for what he is, and to speak from his character and not from his tongue, and which evermore tends to pass into our thought and hand and become wisdom and virtue and power and beauty. We live in succession, in division, in parts, in particles. Meantime within man is the soul of the whole; the wise silence; the universal beauty, to which every part and particle is equally related; the eternal ONE. And this deep power in which we exist and whose beatitude is all accessible to us, is not only self-sufficing and perfect in every hour, but the act of seeing and the thing seen, the seer and the spectacle, the subject and the object, are one. We see the world piece by piece, as the sun, the moon, the animal, the tree; but the whole, of which these are the shining parts, is the soul. Only by the vision of that Wisdom can the horoscope of the ages be read, and by falling back on our better thoughts, by yielding to the spirit of prophecy which is innate in every man, we can know what it saith. Every man's words who speaks from that life must sound vain to those who do not dwell in the same thought on their own part. I dare not speak for it. My words do not carry its august sense; they fall short and cold. Only itself can inspire whom it will, and behold! their speech shall be lyrical, and sweet, and universal as the rising of the wind. Yet I desire, even by profane words, if I may not use sacred, to indicate the heaven of this deity and to report what hints I have collected of the transcendent simplicity and energy of the Highest Law.

If we consider what happens in conversation, in reveries, in remorse, in times of passion, in surprises, in the instructions of dreams, wherein often we see ourselves in masquerade—the droll disguises only magnifying and enhancing a real element and forcing it on our distant notice—we shall catch many hints that will broaden and lighten into knowledge of the secret of nature. All goes to show that the soul in man is not an organ, but animates and exercises all the organs; is not a function, like the power of memory, of calculation, of comparison, but uses these as hands and feet; is not a faculty, but a light; is not the intellect or the will, but the master of the intellect and the will; is the background of our being, in which they lie—an immensity not possessed and that cannot be possessed. From within or from behind, a light shines through us upon things and makes us aware that we are nothing, but the light is all. A man is the façade of a temple wherein all wisdom and all good abide. What we commonly call man, the eating, drinking, planting, counting man, does not, as we know him, represent himself, but misrepresents himself. Him we do not respect, but the soul, whose organ he is, would he let it appear through his action, would make our knees bend. When it breathes through his intellect, it is genius; when it breathes through his will, it is virtue; when it flows through his affection, it is love. And the blindness of the intellect begins when it would be something of itself. The weakness of the will begins when the individual would be something of himself. All reform aims in some one particular to let the soul have its way through us; in other words, to engage us to obey.

Of this pure nature every man is at some time sensible. Language cannot paint it with his colors. It is too subtile. It is undefinable, unmeasurable; but we know that it prevades and contains us. We know that all spiritual being is in man. A wise old proverb says, "God comes to see us without bell"; that is, as there is no screen or ceiling between our heads and the infinite heavens, so is there no bar or wall in the soul, where man, the effect, ceases, and God, the cause, begins. The walls are taken away. We lie open on one side to the deeps of spiritual nature, to the attributes of God. Justice we see and know, Love, Freedom, Power. These natures no man ever got above, but they tower over us, and most in the moment when our interests tempt us to wound them.

The sovereignty of this nature whereof we speak is made known by its independency of those limitations which circumscribe us on every hand. The soul circumscribes all things. As I have said, it contradicts all experience. In like manner it abolishes time and space. The influence of the senses has in most men overpowered the mind to that degree that the walls of time and space have come to look real and insurmountable; and to speak with levity of these limits is, in the world, the sign of insanity. Yet time and space are but inverse measures of the force of the soul. The spirit sports with time—

> Can crowd eternity into an hour,
> Or stretch an hour to eternity.

We are often made to feel that there is another youth and age than that which is measured from the year of our natural birth. Some thoughts always find us young, and keep us so. Such a thought is the love of the universal and eternal beauty. Every man parts from that contemplation with the feeling that it rather belongs to ages than to mortal life. The least activity of the intellectual powers redeems us in a degree from the conditions of time. In sickness, in languor give us a strain of poetry or a profound sentence, and we are refreshed; or produce a volume of Plato or Shakspeare, or remind us of their names, and instantly we come into a feeling of longevity. See how the deep divine thought reduces centuries and millenniums, and makes itself present through all

ages. Is the teaching of Christ less effective now than
it was when first his mouth was opened? The empha-
sis of facts and persons in my thought has nothing to
do with time. And so always the soul's scale is one,
the scale of the senses and the understanding is another. Before the revelations of the soul, Time,
Space and Nature shrink away. In common speech
we refer all things to time, as we habitually refer the
immensely sundered stars to one concave sphere.
And so we say that the Judgment is distant or near,
that the Millennium approaches, that a day of certain political, moral, social reforms is at hand, and
the like, when we mean that in the nature of things
one of the facts we contemplate is external and fugitive, and the other is permanent and connate with
the soul. The things we now esteem fixed shall, one
by one, detach themselves like ripe fruit from our
experience, and fall. The wind shall blow them none
knows whither. The landscape, the figures, Boston,
London, are facts as fugitive as any institution past,
or any whiff of mist or smoke, and so is society, and
so is the world. The soul looketh steadily forwards,
creating a world before her, leaving worlds behind
her. She has no dates, nor rites, nor persons, nor
specialties nor men. The soul knows only the soul;
the web of events is the flowing robe in which she is
clothed. . . .

Revelation is the disclosure of the soul. The popular notion of a revelation is that it is a telling of fortunes. In past oracles of the soul the understanding
seeks to find answers to sensual questions, and un-
dertakes to tell from God how long men shall exist,

what their hands shall do and who shall be their
company, adding names and dates and places. But
we must pick no locks. We must check this low curiosity. An answer in words is delusive; it is really no
answer to the questions you ask. Do not require a
description of the countries towards which you sail.
The description does not describe them to you, and
to-morrow you arrive there and know them by in-
habiting them. Men ask concerning the immortality
of the soul, the employments of heaven, the state of
the sinner, and so forth. They even dream that Jesus
has left replies to precisely these interrogatories.
Never a moment did that sublime spirit speak in
their *patois*. To truth, justice, love, the attributes of
the soul, the idea of immutableness is essentially associated. Jesus, living in these moral sentiments,
heedless of sensual fortunes, heeding only the manifestations of these, never made the separation of the
idea of duration from the essence of these attributes,
nor uttered a syllable concerning the duration of the
soul. It was left to his disciples to sever duration
from the moral elements, and to teach the immortality of the soul as a doctrine, and maintain it by evidences. The moment the doctrine of the immortality
is separately taught, man is already fallen. In the
flowing of love, in the adoration of humility, there is
no question of continuance. No inspired man ever
asks this question or condescends to these evidences.
For the soul is true to itself, and the man in whom it
is shed abroad cannot wander from the present,
which is infinite, to a future which would be finite.

These questions which we lust to ask about the

future are a confession of sin. God has no answer for them. No answer in words can reply to a question of things. It is not in an arbitrary "decree of God," but in the nature of man, that a veil shuts down on the facts of to-morrow; for the soul will not have us read any other cipher than that of cause and effect. By this veil which curtains events it instructs the children of men to live in to-day. The only mode of obtaining an answer to these questions of the senses is to forego all low curiosity, and, accepting the tide of being which floats us into the secret of nature, work and live, work and live, and all unawares the advancing soul has built and forged for itself a new condition, and the question and the answer are one. . . .

Ineffable is the union of man and God in every act of the soul. The simplest person who in his integrity worships God, becomes God; yet for ever and ever the influx of this better and universal self is new and unsearchable. It inspires awe and astonishment. How dear, how soothing to man, arises the idea of God, peopling the lonely place, effacing the scars of our mistakes and disappointments! When we have broken our god of tradition and ceased from our god of rhetoric, then may God fire the heart with his presence.

Format by C. Linda Dingler
Set in Times Roman
Composed, printed and bound by Colonial Press Inc.
HARPER & ROW, PUBLISHERS, INCORPORATED